W9-CCY-007

FOREWORD

Cooperation, the act of working together for one end, is a skill that most parents value highly. Yet, many of us feel sadly lacking when our children are squabbling or resist requests we make of them. How do we teach children to cooperate? Elizabeth Crary's position is that problem solving skills are necessary to learning cooperation and that problem solving is a teachable skill from early ages.

In this book she leads us through several methods and levels of problem solving with many realistic examples. Ms. Crary focuses always on guiding the children toward socially appropriate behavior. Sometimes siblings cooperate effectively to get a grown up's attention by quarrelling. The author suggests numerous helpful ways to redirect those cooperative skills towards problem resolution that meets the needs of all the people involved in the situation.

This is a straight-forward book that offers hands-on help to parents in everyday situations. Rather than focus on the roles children play within the complexity of the family systems, it stays with three easily identifiable reasons why children quarrel. This approach provides a framework for teaching problem solving skills. Following this method carefully, without criticism or manipulation, can be very supportive to a positive family atmosphere. Parents can improve or add these important skills to their repertoire of child rearing methods.

I believe that this is a much needed, helpful book.

Jean Illsley-Clarke, author of *Self-Esteem: A Family Affair*

KIDS CAN COOPERATE

A practical guide to teaching problem solving

by Elizabeth Crary

The author gratefully acknowledges the help of class members, friends and family in the development and editing of this book.

I am particularly thankful the following people for examples or feedback: Patti Buffington, Jean Illsley Clarke, Fred Crary, Lora and Charles Deinken, Nat Houtz, Mary Lynn Hanley, Maggie Lawrence, Linda Meyer, Ann Nachtigal, Ellen Peterson, and Mary Willy.

Copyright © 1984 by Elizabeth Crary
All rights reserved
Printed in the United States

Illustrations copyright © 1984 by Marina Megale

Sorry™ and Survive™ are registered trademarks of the Parker Brothers, division of CPG Products Corp., Beverly, MA 01915.

Dungeons and Dragons™ is a registered trademark owned by TSR, Inc.

ISBN 943990-04-1 (paper)
ISBN 943990-05-X (lib. binding)

LC 84-060587

Parenting Press, Inc.
7750 31st Ave NE
P.0. Box 15163
Seattle WA 98115

TABLE OF CONTENTS

CHAPTER 1: WHEN KIDS QUARREL —

"Mom, he hit me." "She hit me first." "He knocked down my blocks." "She pushed me." "He was in my way...." On and on it goes with each child justifying his or her own behavior. Why do kids fight? Is quarrelling harmful, and what can a parent do short of separating them permanantly or spanking them soundly to reduce the quarrelling? We will look at these questions in this chapter.

The term *sibling rivalry* brings two sets of images to my mind. First is the constant hassle, quibbling or fighting that siblings often engage in. And second is rivalry or competition for parental attention or affection. In this book the term sibling rivalry will include both general bickering and fighting to get parental attention. Most parents will agree that sibling rivalry is the "pits." The constant bickering and fighting is demoralizing—for the parents, if not for the children.

IS SIBLING RIVALRY HARMFUL?

Is sibling rivalry harmful? Maybe, maybe not; it depends upon the situation. Sibling rivalry is harmful when it is verbally or physically abusive or when it gets in the way of normal living. Quarrelling can be useful when it helps children meet their needs and encourages them to grow. Unpleasant as the fighting is for adults, children often get a payoff or benefit from it.

WHY KIDS QUARREL

Let us look at what benefits children may gain from sibling rivalry. Quarrelling can help children gain (1) parental attention, (2) companionship, and (3) a sense of power. We will consider each of these functions in more detail and look at some ways parents can help children meet their needs without quarrelling.

Parental Attention

Parental Attention

Most parents are aware that children may squabble as a way of getting adult attention. Children are adept at raising the conflict level until an adult comes and intervenes. This can be seen in the following example.

Sally and Amy were sitting together drawing pictures. Mom decided to take advantage of the quiet to make a few phone calls. After a while Amy wanted the color marker that Sally was using. When Sally refused to give it to her, Amy "accidentally" bumped her. Sally complained, but there was no adult response. Then Amy grabbed the crayon away "because Sally had it too long." Sally howled and grabbed it back, but there was still no adult response. Next Amy hit Sally. Finally Sally's cry, "She hit me," brought a parent.

This kind of quarrelling drives most parents crazy. However, there are four things a parent can do to decrease the need for children to use quarrelling as an attention-getting device:

Give each child some special time. Research shows that 20 minutes of attention per day dramatically reduces whining and aggressive behavior. To be most effective, the special time should be regular, one-to-one, with an activity chosen by the child. (Special time is not the time for parents to teach or lecture the child.) Preschoolers need time each day. Teenagers may prefer longer weekly blocks.

Your experience can guide you. Parents often worry about where they will find the extra time to spend with their children. Interestingly enough, most parents find that when they give the time willingly, children need less time, and so the parents actually gain time.

Recognize each child's uniqueness or individuality. Many parents try very hard to treat their children equally. Somehow though, it is not possible to be exactly equal. The harder a parent tries, the more deviations are seen as favoritism. It is my observation that most children would rather be seen as special. To do this, parents can look at their children, see what individual talents or interests they have, and encourage those areas. When discussing uniqueness, avoid labels and judgmental comparisons, like "our best student" or "the fastest soccer player." Judgments tend to increase competitive feelings between children and limit children to their current behavior. Labels can be replaced by descriptive statements like "Mary is studying hard to become a veterinarian," or "David runs very fast."

Teach children to ask for attention constructively. Children use quarrelling as a means of getting adult attention because it works. Parents can invite children to ask for attention directly. (For example: "If you want attention or loving, you can come and ask for it.") When you extend this invitation, you need to be willing to give them attention when they ask, especially in the beginning while a new habit is being formed.

Parents have a choice in *how* their child gets attention, not *whether* they get it. A parent can decide how she wants her child to ask for attention, and give attention when appropriate. For example, one toddler raises his arms and grunts, another child comes and asks for a story. With children it is particularly important to respond quickly when teaching a new behavior. After the habit is established, there is more room for variation.

Imagine the child as you want him or her to behave. If you want your children to cooperate, think of what that would be like. Imagine the stages children will go through as they learn to cooperate. Research consistently indicates that people see what they expect to see. If parents believe their children are quarrelsome, they will see their children quarrelling. If they think of their children as learning to cooperate, they will be able to see times when they cooperate.

Parents can encourage children to continue trying to cooperate by noticing their attempts, even if they are not completely successful. The encouragement can be non-verbal (like a smile) or verbal (like praise). For example, Mom could say, "Jimmy, I noticed you stop and think about what to do when Sara called you a dummy."

Quarrelling for Companionship

When children are toddlers they are primarily interested in exploring their world. As they grow older, they are interested in the companionship of other children. At first this takes the form of watching other children or using children as things. Next, they play near other children, and finally playing with them becomes more common.

Some children are skillful at getting others to play with them, while other children quarrel as a way of interacting with their siblings. If a child has tried unsuccessfully several times to involve a sibling in an activity, he can almost always involve them by starting a fight. The results may look unpleasant from the adult viewpoint but may be better than being alone for the child. This can be seen in the following example.

Molly (age 3) wanted to play with her older brother John. John (age 8) had received a new toy for his birthday and was trying to play with it. Molly had tried several approaches—asked him to read to her, asked him to play ball with her and asked what he was doing. All attempts were brushed aside. Finally, out of boredom, she kicked his new toy and ran away. Predictably John got up and chased after her with the intent to "get her."

Parents can reduce quarrelling as a way to gain companionship by structuring the environment to reduce conflicts, teaching children how to ask to play, and finding additional playmates.

Structure the environment to reduce conflicts. Structuring the environment has two components: providing enough space and providing suitable activities. It is easier for children to play cooperatively if they have enough space.

Adults can provide suitable activities by collecting games and activities that children of different ages can participate in. With wide age differences it is more challenging to find activities children can enjoy together. Some activities children can share are blocks, climbing equipment, art supplies (paper, paint, glue, glitter, stickers, etc.), puppets, and dress up clothes. As children grow older, board games, cards and sports can be fun for various ages. Board games are usually more fun if they involve a large amount of chance, for example, Sorry™, Survive™ or checkers.

Parents may need to teach school-age children that preschoolers make their own rules, cannot cope with losing and are not, at age five, "cheating" in the grown-up sense when they deviate from the rules. Parents can also help establish "handicaps" that will even out the age and experience gap, and permit them to play more evenly. For example, in Chinese Checkers six year old Mark takes two moves for each of 12 year old Matt's.

Sports are also more successful if the younger children are given an advantage to offset their inexperience. Another way to help preschoolers play cooperatively is to provide a space large enough so that children can play near each other without getting in each other's way.

Teach children to recognize feelings of others. Children can be taught to observe whether their brother or sister likes the activity they are involved in. Because of their egocentric nature, children are often unaware of how others feel. Parents can teach children to look at facial expressions and body language, and to listen to sounds to get information. Below are two examples.

Sara (age 3½) was an affectionate child. However sometimes she got carried away with her hugs. Mother came in to see her hugging her sister Norma (age 2) who was struggling to get free. Mother said, "Sara, look at Norma's face. Does she like that hug?"

Matt (age 4½) and Evan (age 2½) were yelling and rough housing. At first it was fun for both. Then Evan wanted to stop and began to cry in earnest. Mom came in and asked, "Matt, is this game fun for Evan too?" Matt said he didn't know. Mother replied, "Look at his expression. Does he look like he is having fun? Listen to his voice. Does it sound like he is having fun?"

When parents tell their children to stop or that someone is unhappy, children learn to rely on others for that type of information. When parents consistently ask children to observe other children's feelings and show them how to observe, they offer a skill that will be useful throughout life.

Teach children how to involve others. This can involve helping children negotiate a time to play together, or teaching them how to include other children in their activity. Two examples in which children involve others are described below.

Mark (age 4) wanted to play with his sister, Jenny (age 5). Jenny was stuffing envelopes for her mother and wanted to continue. Finally Jenny thought of asking Mark to pass her the envelopes one at a time so she could stuff them.

Paul (age 6) wanted to play with his older brother, Eric (age 10). Paul proposed playing space invaders, club house and checkers. However Eric wanted to plan characters for a Dungeons and Dragons™ game. After some negotiation they decided to have a Dungeons and Dragons™ Club meeting in Paul's room, where Eric would plan his characters and Paul would help him as needed.

Find some additional playmates so the burden of "entertainment" does not always fall on the sibling. Other families with children can be found in local parks, preschools, youth groups and babysitting co-ops. When you find a child of appropriate age and interests, invite him or her over.

Quarrelling for Power

Some children initiate fights just to see how much power they have over another child. Sometimes the desire for power takes the form of forcing someone to do something. At other times it involves getting the other child in trouble (e.g., pestering a sibling until she hits him and then having the parent punish her). This is illustrated in the following example.

Matthew (age 6) and Geoffry (age 3½) were watching TV. Geoffry was tired of watching the show and wanted to see a different show. The family rule was that the channel could not be turned while someone else was watching it. Geoffry asked if he could turn the TV off so he could change the channel but Matt said he was watching the show. Geoffry began to talk loudly and bump his brother "accidentally" until Matt hit him. Geoffry wailed in a loud voice, "Mommy, Matt hit me." Mother, entering at that moment, scolded Matt and sent him to his room. Then she comforted "poor" Geoffry. When she left, Geoffry turned on the show he wanted to watch.

One of the benefits a child gets from having a sibling is the chance to experiment and see how much power she has and how she can use that power. Personally, I think it is desirable when that experimenting takes place at home where parents can monitor it. However, sometimes the desire for power gets out of hand. When that happens there are several things parents can do to reduce the quarrelling.

Decline to apportion blame unless you see the whole situation. When a parent arrives after the battle has begun, it is often wise to resolve the current problem while declining to find fault. It is surprising how many young children provoke their older siblings to hit them so they will get them in trouble. One way to intervene without taking sides is to focus on the future rather than on the past. When a child says, "It wasn't my fault, he started it," the parent can reply "I don't care who started it. Let's look at your options now. What do you need to be able to play pleasantly together?"

Give children age-appropriate affirmations. Jean Illsley Clarke in her book, *Self Esteem: A Family Affair,* lists affirmations that children need at different ages. All the affirmations revolve around being lovable and capable. Children who feel powerful do not need to continually prove they are powerful by quarrelling with others. Below are several affirmations I find particularly helpful for children experimenting with power.

For 18 months to 3 year olds: "I'm not afraid of your anger." And, "You can think about what you feel."

For 3 to 6 year olds: "You don't have to act scared, sick, mad or sad to get your needs met." And, "You can ask for what you want directly."

For 6 to 12 year olds: "It is okay to disagree." And, "You don't have to suffer or be mean to get your needs met."

These affirmations encourage children to feel good about themselves and take responsibility for their behavior.

Encourage negotiation where both children win. When children get into conflict situations, parents can help them talk about what options are available. Parents can also show how other children might feel differently about different options. A method that adults can use to help children learn to negotiate is presented in the next chapter.

Set age-appropriate limits. Age-appropriate limits change as the children grow. With young children, parents need to consistently enforce the rules they feel are important. As children grow, parents can point out the benefits of rules—they protect you as well as protecting the other person. Finally, some children learn to decide what is right for themselves, rather than relying on a set of rules. A challenge for parents is to recognize their children's stages and encourage them to consider the next levels of development.

It is often difficult to understand the motive of a child's behavior without knowing the context. The following exercise will permit you to look at possible motives for quarrelling.

EXERCISE 1-1: Motives for Quarrelling (page 12)

EXERCISE 1-1: Motives for Quarrelling

INSTRUCTIONS: *Read each situation presented below and decide why the children are quarrelling. Suggest a possible response for the parent.*

Situation A: Ricky (age 9) is trying to teach himself to play chess. His brother Adam (age 4) has asked him to play "Star Wars", to build with blocks and to play ball—all with no response. Finally Adam kicks the chess set and runs away. Ricky gets up and chases after him.

Adam's motive probably was _____.

Parent's possible response _____.

Situation B: Emily (age 2½) is looking at pictures in a book. Jessica (age 4) grabs the book and runs to hide behind her mother who is cooking. Emily follows along crying "Mine, mine, mine." Jessica responds "It's my book. You can't have it."

Jessica's motive probably was_____.

Parent's possible response _____.

Situation C: Jason (age 11) and Adam (age 5) are playing quietly in the living room. Jason stops reading and begins to stare at Adam. Adam asks him to stop. Jason ignores his request and continues to stare. "Adam if you don't stop, I'll tell Mommy." Jason continues to stare, and Adam runs off to Mommy.

Jason's motive probably was _____.

Parent's possible response _____.

Possible Answers:

A. Motive — companionship

  Possible parental action:
1. provide a protected place for the older child OR
2. find additional playmates for younger child.

B. Motive — attention

  Possible parental action:
1. provide special time each day OR
2. teach Jessica how to ask for attention.

C. Motive — power

  Possible parental action:
1. help children discuss their problem together, OR
2. offer Jason an affirmation, for example "You are a powerful person, and you find ways _____."

PARENTAL OPTIONS

We have looked at three motives for children's quarrelling (parental attention, companionship and desire for power) and ways parents can reduce quarrelling and help children meet their needs in acceptable ways. Next we will look at options the parent has once fighting has begun.

When children are quarrelling, five things a parent can do are: ignore the behavior, restructure the environment, tell the children what to do, offer them choices, or help them negotiate a solution. Each of the options is appropriate at some times and inappropriate at other times. Let us look briefly at them.

Ignoring. Ignoring is most effective when you both ingore undesirable behavior *and* also give attention to your child when he or she behaves appropriately. A parent ignores children's quarrelling by acting as though the undesirable behavior is not happening. Ignoring includes calm body langauge as well as not speaking or looking. One way some parents keep calm is to fill their mind with calm images and concentrate on those thoughts. Sometimes ignoring is so difficult that a parent may need to leave the area. When the children stop quarrelling and calm returns, the parent encourages cooperation by giving attention when they act pleasantly.

Restructuring the enviroment. There are times when the easiest way to handle a sibling conflict is to arrange the environment so it is not as likely to happen. This can be done by removing things, adding things or changing the way things are arranged. For example, if a school-aged child is very upset with a toddler using his things while he is at school, the simplest solution may be to put those items on a high shelf so they are out of reach of the toddler. Another way to arrange the environment is to make sure you have enough highly desired toys that both children can play.

Directing behavior. When parents direct the situation, they move in and tell the children what to do. Parents can direct behavior in ways that encourage a child's development or in ways that undermine a child's self-esteem. This can be seen in the following examples.

Mark and Paul were quarrelling over whose turn it was to set the table and do the dishes.

Example A: Mother comes in and says, "You boys are obnoxious. All you ever do is quarrel. Next thing I know you will be fighting over who got dressed first this morning. Mark, you set the table. Paul, you do the dishes tonight."

Example B: Mother comes in and says, "I am trying to read. Your noise is bothering me. I know you can find a quieter way to solve your problems. Mark, you set the table on even numbered days. Look at the calandar and see whose day it is to set the table."

Here are three criteria to determine if directions are constructive or destructive:
(1) Does the statement focus on the behavior rather than the personality?
(2) Does the statement tell the child how to succeed rather than how to fail?
(3) Does the statement expect the child to succeed in the future rather than to fail?

When the directions focus on behavior, tell the child how to succeed and expect success, then they are constructive. Look at the two examples above and check the criteria.

Offering choices. Parents can offer choices and let children decide what to do. This approach can help introduce children to a variety of social skills. Offer only choices you are willing to have the children choose. "You can ask Mary for a turn to look at the book, or you can trade for another book." If it is appropriate, the choice can include the undesirable behavior and consequence. For example, "You can decide who gets the book pleasantly, or continue to quarrel and I will remove the book." Offering choices increases children's decision-making ability and their sense of control.

Encouraging negotiation. Adults can encourage negotiation by asking children to identify their problems, to think of alternatives, to predict consequences and to make decisions. We will look at how to teach children to negotiate in more detail in the next chapter. When children have the skills and experience needed, they can usually solve their conflicts themselves.

Let us take a look at the different ways parents may respond to situations.

Examples of Parental Options

Mother is at the dining room table, drinking a cup of coffee and reading the newspaper. Annie and Bobby are playing in the living room. Suddenly a quarrel erupts with the sound of falling blocks and shouting children.

Ignoring. Mother continues to read the newspaper. When the noise increases, she recalls a pleasant trip to the mountains, and focuses on the beautiful, calm lake there. Eventually the children calm down. Mom goes in a few minutes later and says "I'm glad you two are playing together pleasantly. I see that you are building a block tower together."

Restructuring the environment. One way Mom could reduce the number of conflicts children have is to enlarge the space they play in. She could provide more space by removing as much furniture as possible from the living room or moving the blocks outside so there is more space.

Directing behavior. When Mother hears the noise, she goes into the living room. Depending upon her mood she can direct things in different ways. Below are two examples.

Example A:
Mother: What is going on here?
Bobby: Annie hit me.
Annie: He knocked down my blocks.
Mother: Stop fighting. I have had enough. Annie, you go to your room.
        Bobby, put away your trucks and go play outdoors.

Example B:
Mother: What is going on here?
Bobby: Annie hit me.
Annie: He knocked down my blocks.
Mother: Bobby, why did you knock down Annie's blocks?
Bobby: She was taking up too much room.
Mother: Why did you need more room?
Bobby: To drive my trucks.
Mother: Okay, Bobby. You drive your trucks in this half of the room.
        And Annie, you can build over there.

Offering choices might have started out the same way. However instead of telling the children what to do, mother would offer choices.

Mother: What is going on here?
Bobby: Annie hit me.
Mother: Annie, why did you hit Bobby?
Annie: He knocked down my blocks.
Mother: Bobby, why did you knock down Annie's blocks?
Bobby: She was taking up too much room.
Mother: Why did you need more room?
Bobby: To drive my trucks.
Mother: Bobby, you can ask Annie to move her blocks over or drive your trucks in the dining room.

Encouraging negotiation begins by collecting data about what happened and how people feel, and then moves into generating ideas.

Mother: What is going on here?
Bobby: Annie hit me.
Annie: He knocked down my blocks.
Bobby: She was taking up too much room.
Mother: Why did you need more room?
Bobby: To drive my trucks.
Mother: Bobby, how did Annie feel when you knocked down her tower?.
Bobby: Mad.
Mother: How did you feel when Annie hit you?
Bobby: Mad too.
Mother: What can you do so that you can have enough room and Annie won't be mad?
Bobby: I could ask her to play trucks with me.
Mother: What might happen then?
Bobby: She would say no.
Mother: She might say no. What else could you do so you could have enough room and Annie won't be mad?
Bobby: I could ask her to move.
Mother: What might happen if you asked her to move?
Bobby: She would say no.
Mother: She might say no. What else could you do?
Bobby: I could ask her to make roads for me to drive on.
Mother: What might happen then?
Bobby: She might say yes.
Mother: She might say yes. What else can you do so that you have enough room and Annie is happy?
Bobby: I could tell her to go away.
Mother: You could tell her to go away. What might happen then?
Bobby: She wouldn't.
Mother: What else could you do?
Bobby: I don't know.
Mother: You have thought of four ideas. You could ask her to move, you could ask her to play, you could ask her to make roads or you could tell her to go away. Which will you do?
Bobby: Ask her to make roads.

These are examples of five ways adults can respond to children's quarrelling. To decide which approach to use at a given time, adults need to look at their goals for the children involved, the situation, and how they feel at the time. You can practice responding with different options in the following exercise.

EXERCISE 1-2: Identifying Parental Options (page 17)

SUITABILITY OF VARIOUS APPROACHES

Each of the approaches discussed above is appropriate in some situations and not in others. To decide which approach would be most appropriate, consider the purpose of the quarrel, the skills of the children and how you, the adult, feel.

Ignoring quarrelling is appropriate when the children are fighting to get parental attention, when the parent can remain uninvolved, and when the fighting is not physically or emotional harmful to either child.

Restructuring the environment is appropriate when conflict can be eliminated or reduced by changing the physical surroundings. It tends to be more effective if the child's concern is power than if it is parental attention. However, it is not reasonable for parents to get two of everything to reduce quarreling, because this tends to make being "equal" very important and children look for places where the other child received more or better toys.

Directing behavior is appropriate when the situation is unsafe, the children have few social skills, or the parent is too harried to offer choices or help the children negotiate. It is particularly appropriate when the parent needs immediate action. Directing behavior is also appropriate when a child is too tired to make reasonable decisions, or needs "how-to" information on resolving the situation.

Offering choices is appropriate when the situation is safe, and parent has the time to offer choices. Offering choices is not appropriate when the child is out of control, or if there is a particular behavior the parent wants from the child. It is difficult for children to learn to generate ideas if they do not have experience in making choices. Sometimes parents continue to offer choices when their children are capable of solving problems because they are not willing to devote the time necessary to facilitate their problem solving. This approach is a short term gain, but a long term loss.

Encouraging negotiation is appropriate when children have had experience making choices and have the background skills needed. It is not appropriate if there is a particular decision the parent wants from the children or if the parent does not have the time or energy to carry through with the negotiation.

Some parents and teachers are reluctant to begin problem solving with children who are ready because the process appears very time consuming. However, a child who can think of five ways to get something is more likely to get it in a constructive way than a child who can think of only one way. Most adults find that teaching negotiation gains more time in the long run and helps children deal with desires and frustrations more constructively.

EXERCISE 1-3: Options When Kids Quarrel (page 18)

Exercise 1-2: Identifying Parental Options

INSTRUCTIONS: Read the following situation. Read each of the following responses and decide if it illustrates how to ignore, restructure environment, direct the activities, offer choices, or help the children negotiate. Write the type of response in the space preceding the number.

Situation:

It is time for gymnasitic lessons. Mandy (age 5) and Jenny (age 7) rush to the car, each trying to get in the front seat first.

_____ 1. Go back in the house without saying anything.

_____ 2. "Mandy, you sit in the back. Jenny, you sit in the front. On the way home you two will switch."

_____ 3. "Girls, I am tired of hearing you quarrel. You can get in the car pleasantly or we will stay home."

_____ 4. Before the girls go to the car, remove the front passenger seat.

_____ 5. "I can tell you kids have a problem. Both of you want to ride in the front seat now. Let us list the different ways to decide who sits in the front. Mandy, what is one way you can solve the problem?"

_____ 6. "It is time to go. You decide who gets in the front seat or I will decide."

_____ 7. "I will toss a coin. If it land on heads, Mandy is in the front on the way to gymnastics. If it is tails, Jenny will be in the front on the way to gymnastics. On the way home we will switch."

_____ 8. Take a book left in the car, sit down in the driver's seat and begin to read.

_____ 9. "I know you two are capable of working this out. List what you can do and decide what will work for both of you. If you need help, you can ask for it. When you are pleasantly in the car, we can go."

_____ 10. "Be quiet. If I hear one more sound we will all stay home today."

_____ 11. Tell the girls you are all going to take the bus today.

_____ 12. Talk to the neighbor who is out weeding the lawn.

_____ 13. "You can sit in the back, or I will decide who sits in the back."

_____ 14. Prevent either of them from sitting in the front seat by strapping a large box in the front seat.

_____ 15. "Mandy, you can sit in the back. Jenny you read a story to Mandy while we drive to gymnastics."

Answers.

1. Ignore the situation
2. Direct the situation
3. Offer choices
4. Restructure the environment
5. Help children negotiate
6. Offer choices
7. Direct the situation
8. Ignore the situation
9. Encourage children to negotiate
10. Direct the situation
11. Restructure the environment
12. Ignore the situation
13. Offer choices
14. Restructure the environement
15. Direct the situation

EXERCISE 1-3: Options when Kids Quarrel

INSTRUCTIONS: Read the situations and write a possible completion for each option.

Situation:

1. Dad is in the back yard mowing the lawn. Danny and David (both age 5) are quarrelling over whose turn it is to swing. Danny is on the swing, and David is tired of waiting and wants a turn.

   Dad could *ignore* the quarrelling by _____

   _____ .

2. Danny and David continue to fight over whose turn it is to be on the swing.

   Dad could *restructure the environment* by _____

   _____ .

3. David picks up a large stick and tells Danny if he doesn't get off, he will push him off with the stick. Dad decides he will intervene because the situation is unsafe.

   Dad could *direct the situation* by _____

   _____ .

4. David asks Dad for help dealing with Danny. Dad decides to offer David two choices.

   Dad could *offer the choices of:* _____

   OR _____ .

5. Neither ideas Dad offers appeals to David. Dad decides to help the boys negotiate. He could begin by:

   _____

   _____

Possible answers:

1. Ignore: Continuing to mow the lawn, OR weeding out front, OR thinking about taking a trip to Hawaii.
2. Restructure the environment: Removing the swing or putting up another one.
3. Direct situation: Saying "David, put down the stick. It is dangerous. If you need ideas, ask me."
4. Offer choices: Saying "David, you can offer to let him ride your bike, or fill the pool with water and play until he is done."
5. Encourage negotiation: Saying "Boys, I want you to find a way to share the swing that makes you both happy. You may use the swing when you get a plan. What are some ideas?"

Kids Can Cooperate

SIX IDEAS TO PREVENT QUARRELLING

Can quarrelling be prevented? I really don't know. In our culture some "rivalry" is certainly the norm and has been cultivated to support our current competitive mode of business. However, personal experience and observation suggest that the frequency and severity of quarrels can be reduced. The following is a list of six things to do to prevent or reduce quarrelling.

1. GIVE EACH CHILD SOME SPECIAL TIME EACH DAY. Give regular, undivided parental attention focusing on what the child wants to do.

2. TEACH CHILDREN TO ASK FOR ATTENTION CONSTRUCTIVELY. Children will get attention when they need it. Adults can influence how.

3. RECOGNIZE CHILDREN AS INDIVIDUALS. Look for ways each child is special. Avoid judgmental comparisons between children.

4. TEACH CHILDREN HOW TO NEGOTIATE WITH OTHERS. Encourage children to look at alternatives, consequences and how their behavior affects others.

5. STRUCTURE THE ENVIRONMENT TO REDUCE CONFLICT. Provide space and activities so children can play together.

6. VISUALIZE CHILDREN AS COMPETENT AND CARING. Children often act as we think they will. Spend time thinking of them as successful.

In this chapter we have looked at some reasons why children quarrel and five options parents have in dealing with their quarrelling. With four of these options (ignoring, restructuring the enviornment, directing behavior, and offering choices), children are dependent upon the parent to provide or enforce cooperation. The fifth option, encouraging negotiation, permits children to take responsiblity for acting cooperatively. The rest of this book will focus on how adults can help children understand and develop the skills needed to solve their problems themselves. The next chapter introduces the problem solving process more fully and describes how to begin to teach it to children.

CHAPTER 2: HOW TO FACILITATE PROBLEM SOLVING

Children fight because it gets them what they want or because it is all they know. In order to help children stop quarrelling we need to teach them new skills. Problem solving can be taught directly by teaching the negotiation process or indirectly by modeling the skills. In this chapter, we will look at how adults can help children negotiate. Chapter 5 will discuss how parents can model problem solving by negotiating with children during child-parent conflicts.

Is it really possible to teach children to resolve social conflicts? Yes! Research (Spivak and Shure) demonstrates that adults (both parents and teachers) can teach children to solve their own problems. They found that a child's social adjustment (ability to get what he or she wants in an acceptable manner) correlates directly with the number of alternatives the child can think of in a situation and with his or her ability to predict the consequences of those alternatives.

Interestingly, Spivak and Shure found the ability to generate ideas in a social situation was *not* related to the IQ, general creativity, verbal ability or the sex of the child. Some children discover how to negotiate on their own, and others do not. Fortunately, however, Spivak and Shure found they could *teach* the cognitive approach to problem solving. Thus a child who can think of five ways to get what he wants will generally display more socially acceptable behavior than a child who can think of only one or two ways. With this in mind, we will look at the problem solving process, how adults can assist children in negotiating conflicts, and then consider how to introduce the problem solving process to children.

STEPS IN PROBLEM SOLVING.

There are a variety of ways to facilitate problem solving. However, successful approaches have several steps in common: gathering data, defining the problem, generating ideas, evaluating alternatives and asking for a decision.

1. Gather data. When you come in and find your children upset, first find out what happened. Questions like, "What happened? Why did you ... ? What happened then?" are appropriate. When the questions are asked calmly and non-judgmentally, children usually calm down and answer them.

It is also helpful to encourage children to look at the feelings involved. Children, particularly preschoolers, see things primarily from their own perspective. They may be totally unaware of how their behavior affects other people, except when another person interferes with their needs. To negotiate solutions that are fair to everyone, children need to know how others feel. You can help children understand how other people feel by asking them to look at another child and tell you how they think that child feels, or ask them to remember how they felt in a similar situation. Focus on the feelings of *both* children involved in a conflict, not just the "aggressor" or "victim."

2. Define the Problem. Generating alternatives is much easier for children when they have a clear goal. Help your children define a problem in terms of what both children want to happen. For example, "What can you do so you have room to drive your trucks and Annie has room to play with the blocks?" When you phrase the problem this way, children get the idea that *both* children's needs are important.

3. Generate alternatives. The parent's job in assisting children to negotiate is to help them focus on the problem and to act as a "blackboard." To do that, present the problem and wait for your children to suggest alternatives. For example, Ken has been pestering his older brother Luke, who is reading, to play with him. Ken snatches the book and runs. After collecting data, Mom says, "Luke, what can you do so you and Ken can both have fun?"

After your child gives you one idea, repeat it and then ask him what else he could do. For example, "Yes, you could let him use the tiny trucks while you read. What else can you do?"

Resist the temptation to suggest ideas. When an adult suggests ways to handle a conflict, most children assume their own ideas were not good enough. If you think your child needs new ideas, suggest them later; or, ask the child to imagine how someone else they know might handle the situation. For example, "You can't think of any more ideas. What might Jennifer do if she wanted the truck?" Or, "Remember the sharing book. What did Amy do to get the truck?"

4. Evaluate alternatives. After your children have generated all the ideas they can, evaluate the consequences. For example, ask one of them, "What might happen if you grabbed the truck?" or, "How might Jamie feel if you hit him?" If your child has trouble evaluating the ideas, recall a similar situation that happened to him. For example, "Remember when Mark grabbed the ball you were playing with. How did you feel then?"

Resist the temptation to judge the ideas. Fortunately a child's problem solving ability correlates with the number of different ideas she has, not the number of *good* ideas. Parents will not always be around to tell a child that her idea is not good and to suggest another. You will be more helpful in the long run by encouraging your child to evaluate an idea herself and see why it is unacceptable.

5. Ask for a decision. When your child is through thinking of ideas and evaluating ideas, it is time to make a plan. Restate the problem, summarize the ideas and let your child decide on which idea she will try. If your child chooses an alternative that you think will not work, be sure she knows what she will do next. For example, "Amy, you decided to ask Megan to trade dolls. What will you do if she says no?" Amy may reply with anything from "I don't know" to "Sock her." If you think your child will need help you may remind her, "If you need more help you can come and ask me for ideas."

The following are two examples of children's problem solving. In the first example, Dad helped the children through the process; in the second example, the children resolved the problem themselves.

Example 1: Two children (Alice and Becky, ages 4 and 3) are crying. Dad enters and sees books and toys all over.

Dad: What happened?
Alice: Becky pushed me.
Dad: Becky, why did you push Alice?
Becky: She took my drum.
Dad: Alice, why did you take Becky's drum?
Alice: She was making too much noise.

Dad:	Why did you need more quiet?
Alice:	To read my book.
Dad:	Alice, how do you think Becky felt when you grabbed her drum?
Alice:	Mad.
Dad:	How did you feel when Becky pushed you?
Alice:	Mad too.
Dad:	What can you do so that you can read your book and Becky can have fun too?
Alice:	I could ask her to look at books with me.
Dad:	Yes, you could ask her to look at books with you. What might happen then?
Alice:	She'd say no.
Dad:	She might say no. What else could you do so you can read your book and Becky can have fun?
Alice:	Ask her to play quietly.
Dad:	What might happen then?
Alice:	She wouldn't.
Dad:	You could ask her to look at books with you or ask her to play quietly. What else could you do?
Alice:	I could let her play with my rag doll.
Dad:	What might happen then?
Alice:	She might do it.
Dad:	What else could you do?
Alice:	I could ask her to move.
Dad:	What might happen if you asked her to move?
Alice:	She'd say no again.
Dad:	You thought of four ways to get quiet: ask Becky to look at a book while you read, ask her to move, let her play with your rag doll, and ask her to play quietly. Which idea will you try first?
Alice:	Let her play with my rag doll.

Example 2: Two children (Rick 10, Anna 6) are in the back seat of the car, quarrelling over how to use the seat between them.

Rick:	I want to put my books there.
Anna:	I want to put my jacket there.
Rick:	Why do you want to put your jacket there?
Anna:	Because I need some place to put it.
Rick:	Can you put it on the other side of you?
Anna:	No, I'll be too squished. You can put your books on the floor.
Rick:	No. They might get dirty. Can you put your jacket in the front seat?
Anna:	Okay.

The process of teaching problem solving often seems tedious, but it gives children practice thinking up and evaluating alternatives for their own situations. In the examples above, the children were clearly familiar with the procedure of problem solving. Next we will consider some guidelines for helping children solve their problems.

EXERCISE 2-1: Identifying Steps in Problem Solving (page 24)

How to Facilitate

GUIDELINES
FOR
FACILITATING
PROBLEM
SOLVING

Children will learn to resolve conflicts more easily if adults keep these points in mind.

1. Encourage solutions where everyone wins. Help the child focus on people's feelings. The goal is a solution which will allow **everyone** some satisfaction.

2. Avoid criticizing ideas. When a child generates ideas, do not judge the ideas yourself. Part of the assisting role is helping the child to evaluate his own ideas. If a child says, "I could hit Jimmy," say, "Yes, you could hit Jimmy. What might happen then?" rather than "Oh no, we don't hit. That's not nice." If the child comes up with several ideas like hitting and punching and pinching, you can say, "Hitting, punching, and pinching are all hurting ideas. What is something different you can do?" Focus on generating more ideas rather than evaluating the ideas.

3. Focus on children's ideas. Do not offer your ideas while you are helping children negotiate. Parents are often tempted to offer children ideas; however,

---

Exercise 2-1: Identifying Steps in Problem Solving

INSTRUCTIONS: *Read the situation below. Then read the following sections and match each problem solving step (numbered) with the appropriate dialogue (lettered).*

Situation:
Michael (age 7) and Matthew (age 9) are both in the dining room doing their homework on the table. Suddenly there are loud noises coming from the dining room. Both boys are fighting over a pencil.

1. Gather Data

A: 1. I can't think with the radio on either.
    2. Okay
    3. Michael wouldn't keep his pencil still.
    4. I don't want to wear ear muffs inside.
    5. Dad does not want to enforce your rules.
    6. It breaks the family rule of "No TV before homework."

2. Define the Problem

B: Dad goes in and inquires, "Does anyone need first aid?" Both boys reply, "No."
Then Dad says, "Michael tell me why you are upset."
Michael replies, "Matt grabbed my pencil away."
Dad then inquires, "Matt, why are you upset?"
Matt replies, "He was making so much noise with his pencil, I couldn't work."

3. Generate Ideas

C: "You two have a problem. Michael wants to tap his pencil while he studies, and Matt needs quiet while he studies. What can you do so both of you can study?"

4. Evaluate Ideas

D: 1. We could turn on the radio so the tapping wouldn't bother Matt.
    2. I could study in my room and Matt can study at the table.
    3. Michael could stop banging his pencil on the table.
    4. Matt could wear ear muffs so I can do what I want to.
    5. Ask Dad to stay here and make Michael be quiet.
    6. I could watch TV now, and Matt could do homework.

5. Decide and Implement a Plan

E: Michael works at the dining room table. Matt works in his room.

Possible responses:

1. Gather Data: B
2. Define the Problem: C
3. Generate Ideas: D
4. Evaluate Ideas: A
5. Decide on one idea and implement: E

Kids Can Cooperate

if you give children ideas they may assume your ideas are better than theirs or that you do not think they can think of any ideas that are suitable. If you want to expand the alternatives a child can think of, do it later. One constructive way to do that is to role play with puppets or make up a story which brings in some new ideas on how to handle those problems.

4. Review the problem frequently. It is easy for children to become distracted from the problem. To help them focus on the content, repeat the problem statement each time you ask for ideas. For example, "How can you get a turn on the tricycle and still have your friend feel happy?"

5. Act as a "blackboard." Many children have difficulty remembering the ideas they think of and thinking of new ideas at the same time. When adults remember the ideas, children can concentrate on generating ideas. For example, "You could ask him to get off the swing, you could knock him off, or you could go inside and play with the building blocks." Repeating all the ideas each time may seem tedious to parents, but it is important to children because it lets them see the list grow and know that their ideas are important.

6. Focus on content, not grammar. Do not worry about grammar. If the child uses a double negative or gets his sentence scrambled, let it pass. When you summarize the idea you can rephrase it grammatically, but do not ask the child to repeat the correction.

EXERCISE 2-2: Identifying Common Errors (page 26)

COMMON QUESTIONS

When people begin to facilitate problem solving with children, they often have a number of questions. Some of them are discussed below.

"Why do you have to go through all this? Why not just tell my child what to do?" When you tell your child what to do, he does not gain the experience of thinking of what to do for himself. Some children can take information given one time and then generate alternatives for themselves in other situations. Other children have difficulty doing this. They have what might be called 'social blindness'; that is, they cannot see any alternatives in social situations. They see only one idea, and they move forward without considering how that will affect others. Problem solving, or generating alternatives, helps them think of several options so they can find several ways of getting what they want. Then they are more likely to find a way that is successful, a way they can get what they want while allowing other people to be happy too.

"Why keep repeating the problem each time?" It is easy for children to wander from the original problem and get into a second issue, and from that onto another issue without ever having solved anything. When you repeat the problem each time, it refreshes your memory and your child's memory about the problem. The child can focus on the problem better.

"Why not evaluate the ideas as you go?" For some reason, evaluating solutions tends to stop the flow of ideas. That is particularly true if the evaluations are negative. However, when you are first introducing the idea of alternatives and their consequences, it is sometimes easier to evaluate as you go.

"Why repeat all the previous alternatives each time?" One reason for repeating all the choices is so your child can see how the number of alternatives is growing. Another reason is so the child will not suggest the same ideas. It is sometimes

Exercise 2-2: Identifying Common Errors.

INSTRUCTIONS: *Read each section. Identify the error and rewrite the parent's response to avoid that error.*

Situation:

Kelsey (age 5) has been coloring with markers from the family collection. Kate (age 3½) grabbed some markers and started to run away. Kelsey caught her and was trying to get the marking pens back. Mother comes in and decides to help them negotiate.

1. Mother: What is wrong, girls?
    Kelsey: Katie keeps taking the markers away.
    Katie: I want a turn.
    Mother: Looks like you two have a problem. Katie, how can you get a turn with the marking pen?

    Error: _____

    Suggested change: _____

2. Katie: I could hit her and grab it.
    Mother: Oh, no. You wouldn't do that. That is a bad idea. What else could you do?
    Katie: I could ask nicely.
    Mother: Yes, you could ask nicely.

    Error: _____

    Suggested change: _____

3. Mother: You could ask nicely. What else could you do?
    Katie: I don't know.
    Mother: Well, you could play with something else or set the timer.

    Error: _____

    Suggested change: _____

4. Mother: What else could you do?
    Katie: I could let her use my new doll.
    Mother: You mean you could trade your new doll for the markers. Say, "I could trade for the dolls."

    Error: _____

    Suggested change: _____

5. Mother: Katie, you have several ideas: you can ask nicely for the markers, play with a different toy, take turns, or trade. What will you do?

    Error: _____

    Suggested change: _____

Possible answers.

1. Error: Looking for a solution for only one person.
    Change: Both of you want to play with the markers. What can you do so both of you have fun?

2. Error: Criticizing ideas.
    Change: Yes, you could hit her. What might happen then?

3. Error: Suggesting ideas.
    Change: What do you think Jennifer might do if she wanted to play with the markers?
            OR

If you need some ideas, we can read the problem solving book *I Want It* to get some ideas.

4. Error: Focusing on grammar.
    Change: You could trade your doll for the markers. What else could you do?

Kids Can Cooperate

hard for children to remember all their suggestions. If remembering the ideas gets tiring, you can jot them down on paper.

"What should I do if my child chooses a 'bad' solution?" That depends upon why the solution was bad. It can be 'bad' because it won't work or because it is hurtful to another person. If your experience suggests the solution won't work, then let your child try it and develop his own experience. If the idea is hurtful to someone, help him understand how his choice will affect the other child. For example, "You could hit Mark to get the ball. How would Mark feel?" (Wait for a response.) "Right, he would feel angry. What could you do so you could play with the ball and Mark will be happy too?"

If he continues with his choice, you can restate the problem and explain that you will not permit choices that hurt other people. For example, "Biting Jeffy is one way to get the truck but it will hurt him. I will not let you hurt him. What can you do so you can both be happy?"

"When two children are squabbling, how do you decide which child to start with?" I have started with the "aggressor" and with the "victim," and it does not seem to make a difference which child you start with. Your preference at the time is probably as good a guide as any. Initially it is easier to start with the child you are most likely to succeed with. When you get more confident you might choose the child who needs the most practice with problem solving. My feeling is that if either child uses problem solving skills, then the frequency of quarrelling will be less than if neither has problem solving skills.

"Can I use this approach with three or more children?" Yes! You can work with each child separately or you can work with them all as a group. When you work with a group you may wish to establish guidelines for who speaks when to avoid one child dominating the discussion. You can permit children to speak randomly or in turn as you go around the circle. If children speak randomly, let each child who wishes have a turn before someone speaks a second time. If you are problem solving with a large group, as in a class room, you may wish to break the group into a circle of 5 or 6 to look for ideas. When it is time to make a decision, it is important for the adult to check that the solution really works for all the children.

"When can I introduce this method to my children?" Many children are able to understand and think of alternatives between three and four years of age, if they have been introduced to the concept. However, most children under seven have difficulty predicting consequences of situations they have not experienced.

"How can you introduce this method to children?" It is best to introduce the problem solving technique when everyone is calm. You can introduce it through a story or puppet plays, and then have the children help the puppets or story characters solve their problems. When the child understands the procedure, then begin using the problem solving technique for their conflicts. When you start using problem solving, begin in a situation where the children are not hysterical and there is still some degree of calm.

5. Error: Not evaluating ideas.
    Change: What might happen if you asked nicely? (Wait.)
            What might happen if you ... ? (Continue until all ideas are evaluated.)
                AND
    Error: Not reviewing goals.
    Change: Well Katie, what can you do so both you and Kelsey can have fun?

"If my children are fighting over a toy, should I take it away?" Let your intuition be your guide. Sometimes it works better if you remove the toy. However, if your child or children can focus on the problem while the toy is present, then it does not matter.

"Can these techniques work for parent-child conflicts as well?" Yes, they can. However, one caution is that you must be very sure both your concerns *and* your child's concerns are considered. Sometimes parents are tempted to use problem solving in an attempt to bring the child around to their preconceived notions. When parents do that, they undermine the basic idea rather than encourage true problem solving.

"What if a child won't cooperate?" If a child won't cooperate, you always have the option of directing the situation or offering choices. One approach that often works is to say, "Do you want to cooperate or shall I decide what will happen?" Most children will choose to have some control.

One of the most important and challenging jobs of a parent is to teach children how to treat other people. Currently in our culture, this is a confusing job both for parents and for children. As a society we believe in being strong and standing up for ourselves; however, we also believe in being polite, cooperative and sharing. The parent or caregiver's job is to make sense of these conflicting values for our children and to teach them skills that reflect our own values. One skill that is both assertive and cooperative is negotiation or problem solving.

Teaching problem solving, as with all types of teaching, begins with finding out what skills the child has. Next we will look at what skills children need, and how to assess those skills. (Looking at the skills is particularly important when you wish to teach children problem solving.) Then we will look at how to introduce the idea of problem solving, and how to provide opportunities to practice.

ASSESSING SKILLS NEEDED FOR PROBLEM SOLVING

There are three skills that children need before they can learn to solve social conflicts: the ability to listen, the use of certain language concepts, and understanding of certain emotional concepts.

Ability to listen. Problem solving is based on the communication of ideas and feelings. In order to communicate, a person must listen and pay attention to others. Children with undiagnosed hearing loss or the inability to focus on what another person is saying will have difficulty negotiating.

Essential language concepts. Problem solving is based on generating ideas and evaluating consequences of those ideas. This process is much easier when children understand basic language concepts. For example, the concepts of "or," "and," "is/is not," and "same/different" help children generate a variety of ideas. Concepts like "if/then," "why/because," and "maybe" help children look at causal relationships between their actions and those of other people. Children also need to know that an item or person can have multiple attributes. For example, a person can be a son, brother and friend, or a person can be glad you are visiting and mad you grabbed his truck.

Understanding feelings. Children who understand how other people feel can solve conflicts more easily than those who do not. Understanding feelings involves identifying feelings, understanding the nature of feelings, and distinguishing between feelings and actions.

Identifying feelings involves both noticing and labeling feelings. To label feelings, children need a feeling vocabulary which includes a range of words for both pleasant feelings (e.g., proud, excited, loved) and unpleasant feelings (e.g., sad, lonely, scared, disappointed). Children also need to know ways to find out how people feel. Most children collect information with their eyes and ears. However, it is important for children to know they can also ask other people how they feel.

Understanding the nature of feelings involves knowing that feelings are personal and that feelings change. Each person has his own feelings. Those feelings are not right or wrong, good or bad, they just are. This includes the idea that different people feel differently about the same thing. For example, not all children like vanilla ice cream, nor do they all like to swing on swings. In addition to being personal, feelings change over time. Just because a friend is mad in the morning does not mean he will be mad forever. Further, people like different things at different times. A child who has played hide and seek all morning may want to play something different after lunch.

Children can learn to distinquish between feelings and actions. Feelings are okay, but some ways of expressing them are not. For example, it is okay to be mad at someone, but not okay to hit her. When children separate feelings and actions, they are in a better position to generate and evaluate different ways to respond. These concepts assist children to negotiate by helping them see a situation from another person's perspective.

How to assess child's understanding. Sometimes it is hard to decide whether a child has the needed skills for problem solving. This is particularly true with preschoolers. A series of "games" are provided in Appendix A which can be used to assess a child's prerequisite skills. These assessment games are designed to be fun for children. Choose a time to play them when you and your child are in a good humor and you have plenty of time. Although the games have been designed for children younger than eight, they may be used with older children if you tell the child you know they are silly questions but you want to begin at the beginning.

Remember that the purpose of the games is to find what level to begin teaching at, rather than to make a judgment about the child. Once you have found out what skills your children need, you can find ways to introduce the skills to them. Activities that promote the basic skills needed are provided in Appendix B. When children understand the basic skills, then you can introduce the concepts needed for problem solving.

INTRODUCE THE PROBLEM SOLVING PROCEDURE

Problem solving is based on two skills: (1) the ability to think of alternatives and (2) the ability to evaluate the consequences of different ideas. For most children it is easier to learn to generate alternatives before learning to predict their consequences.

Model looking at alternatives. The easiest way to introduce the concept of "alternatives" is by modeling it. Amazingly enough, most parents, even those who consciously look for alternatives, rarely explain or model the process. Many children do not know people can look for alternatives in conflict situations. This is clearly illustrated in the following experience of one parent.

I can clearly recall the time I realized I did not verbalize looking for alternatives. I had been working with my 10 year old son, Kevin, for several months, trying to get him to think of alternatives in situations with his younger brother, Mark.

One particularly trying afternoon I blew my cool and sent my children to their rooms. When I calmed down slightly, I thought of several ways I could have better handled the situation. I went to Kevin's room and told him I had handled the situation poorly and listed four ways I could have handled it better. He looked at me with amazement and asked "You have to hunt for alternatives too?" I realized that I had not verbalized the process of looking at alternatives even though I insisted he do so.

Generating alternatives can also be modeled by listing the alternatives you are considering at the time of conflict. For example:

I was disturbed by my children's increasingly noisy fights. I went over to my children who were fighting over a toy and reviewed my alternatives. "There is so much fighting and noise that I can't concentrate. Let me see, what can I do? I can send the children to their rooms, I can ask them to play quietly, I can take the truck away, I can tell them to play in the basement, or I can go to my room and read. I wonder what I should do?" To my amazement the children responded, "Go read, Mom. We can solve it," and they did.

Use books to introduce alternatives. Children's stories can be used directly and indirectly. They can be used directly if they introduce a variety of alternatives and offer the chance to make decisions. A series that introduces alternatives to children is the Children's Problem Solving Series: *I Want It, I Can't Wait, I Want to Play* and *My Name is Not Dummy.* Each of these books begins by introducing a conflict and then listing seven or eight things a child could do. For example, in *I Want It,* Amy wants the truck Megan has. She can grab it, ask for it, trade for it, make a deal, wait for it, threaten or get help. Your child can decide what Amy will do and can see how this situation turns out.

Books can also be used indirectly as a springboard for discussion. When children get accustomed to thinking about alternatives, you can use almost any book to generate discussion. You can do that by beginning the story and stopping after the problem has been presented. Ask your child what the problem is and what the character could do. After your child is through thinking of alternatives, you can go on and read what the characters actually do. Several of the "Serendipity Books" such as *Loopy, Wheedle on the Needle,* and *Creole,* are easy books to begin with.

The ability of children to use a story as a springboard can be seen in the following example.

The children were preparing to act out "The Three Billy Goats Gruff" in circle time. The first billy goat had been warned not to cross the bridge but he was tempted by the green grass on the other side. As he walked up to the bridge, one boy in the class piped up, "Why doesn't he swim across?" Another child picking up the lead said, "He could fly." For several minutes the children talked about ways the billy goat could get green grass without crossing the bridge.

When you and your child get accustomed to making up and evaluating alternatives, you can make up your own stories to reflect the concerns you face.

Introduce alternative thinking with puppets. Many children enjoy watching and talking with puppets. Puppets can be easily used to introduce both the *concept* of alternatives and *a variety* of alternatives. You can begin by having the puppets squabbling over a toy. Then you can talk with the puppets and help them define their problem and look for alternatives. Initially introduce only three or four alternatives at a time. Be sure to watch your children and stop the 'show' before it becomes boring. When your children understand the concept of alternatives and can think of several alternatives, then the puppets can begin to ask your children for help in thinking of ideas and predicting what might happen for each alternative.

Discuss actions and consequences on television. The television can easily be used as the spring board for discussions of alternatives and consequences. Very few television programs show characters considering actions before acting, and in many shows the method of solving differences is through power or force. When you watch a show with a child you can identify the problem and offer alternative ways of handling the situation. The following is an example.

Mom and Annie (age 6) were watching Super Friends on television. At the height of confusion Superman said that they did not have time to think, they needed to act immediately. Mom said, "Not true. When time is short, it is important to think of your alternatives so you can do the fastest one."

Four ways to introduce the problem solving process to children are presented above. Once you get started you will probably find more ways to introduce alternatives to your child. When children have been introduced to different ways to handle situations, you can help them understand the problem solving process by providing situations where they can practice thinking of ideas and evaluating them. Later, after they have had practice in informal situations, you can begin to intervene in their conflicts.

PROVIDE OPPORTUNITY FOR PRACTICE

Once children understand alternatives, and that different behaviors have different consequences, you can begin to help children negotiate when they have quarrels. It is easier for children to begin problem solving when they are not emotionally involved. For many people the simplest ways to introduce problem solving are, as previously mentioned, with puppets or by recalling events that happened to other people. As children gain experience with "other peoples' problems," you can intervene in their conflict and ask them to use the same process for themselves.

Levels of learning. Learning takes place in three predictable stages: recognition, understanding and application. With the first level, recognition, children recall having heard the term or concept before. If they can define the concept, it will be the same explanation they were given. For example, if you asked, "What is an alternative?" they might respond with the same words you used. But if you read them a story illustrating alternatives and asked them to identify one, they could not tell you.

The second level of learning is understanding. After they understand, children can explain concepts or ideas in their own language. For example, if you asked, "What is an alternative?" a six year old child might ask, "For what?" and then list alternatives, or an older child might say, "Something you can do instead of something else." If you read a story illustrating alternatives, the child could identify the alternatives.

The third level of learning is application. At the application stage a child can use the concept. Not only can the child explain and identify alternatives, she can think of them when she needs them. The goal of teaching problem solving is to bring children into the application stage. In some cases it takes longer than others. The process is often made easier by the use of puppets.

Using puppets. Using puppets for application is a natural extension of introducing the concepts with puppets. It is often fun for children to take on the role of 'helper' for the puppets and help them solve a conflict. The child can also use puppets to act out how to play. This is particularly useful if another child plays with the other puppet so the puppets need to negotiate. You can suggest plots that use common conflict situations for those children.

Recalling a previous conflict. Parents and teachers can help a child apply the problem solving ideas by talking about situations that are past. Do this by recalling the incident in a nonjudgmental way, and ask what might have happened if someone did or said something different. To recall a situation nonjudgmentally, focus on the events, not how you felt about it. The following example illustrates both a judgmental and nonjudgmental introduction.

Mom was recalling a dispute between two children earlier in the day.

Situation 1: "Christina, I was really disappointed in how you behaved toward Nicole this morning. I want you to tell me a better way to handle situations like that."

Situation 2: "Christina, remember this morning when you and Nicole were fighting over the doctor kit and I took it away? (Christina nods.) Well, I would like for us to list several other ways you could have handled the situation."

Parents can help children imagine consequences of different ideas by recalling situations and asking "What might happen if ... ". For example (continuing the situation above):

Mom:	When I came in, you were pulling the doctor kit away from Nicole. What else did you think of doing?
Chris:	Hit her and punch her.
Mom:	What might happen if you hurt Nicole?
Chris:	She would get you.
Mom:	You thought of grabbing and hurting. What else could you do?
Chris:	I could ask her to give it to me.
Mom:	What might happen then?
Chris:	She'd say NO!
Mom:	You could grab, or hurt or ask. What else could you do?
Chris:	I don't know.
Mom:	What might Susie do if she wanted the doctor kit?
Chris:	I don't know.
Mom:	What did she do this morning when she wanted the fire truck?
Chris:	She traded for an ambulance.
Mom:	Does that give you any ideas?
Chris:	Yeah, I could trade for something.
Mom:	What might happen if you offered to trade something?
Chris:	It might work, if it was something good.

When children have the skills needed to negotiate, understand the concepts of alternatives and consequences, and have had a chance to practice solving problems for other people, you can help your children to use them in a quarrel.

FIRST TIME ASSISTANCE

Most children find it more difficult to apply the problem solving process to their own quarrels than to use the process to help others. You can make it easier for your child by carefully choosing the time to begin. Avoid times when one of the children is tired, hungry, sick or particularly irritable, and times when you are irritable or rushed. Once children see how the process works, you can expand to other times.

Check list for first intervention

1. Do children have:
   a. The basic skills needed (ability to listen, cognitive ability, and understand feelings)?
   b. An introduction to a variety of alternatives?
   c. Practice in generating ideas and evaluating them using puppets' or other people's conflicts?
2. Has the adult:
   a. Read the section on steps in problem solving? (page 21)
   b. Read how to start problem solving? (page 29)
3. Is the timing appropriate?
   a. The children are not hungry, tired or sick.
   b. The adult has the time and energy to assist with negotiation.
   c. The adult is feeling accepting and supportive.

Summary of steps in intervention. There are five steps for intervention: stop and gather data, identify and define the problem, generate ideas, evaluate ideas then choose one, and plan implementation of the idea.

1. *Gather data* — Find out what happened. How do the children feel about what happened? Do not blame anyone.

2. *Define the problem* — Clearly state the problem. Think in terms of how both (or all) children can meet their needs.

3. *Encourage children to generate ideas* — Act as a blackboard. Avoid judging ideas. Help children keep focused on the problem.

4. *Help children evaluate ideas* — Ask children "What might happen if ..." for each of the ideas. If possible, help them see there are several "mights" for each idea.

5. *Ask for a decision and help plan implementation* — Restate the problem, summarize the alternatives and consequences, and ask for a decision. Help children plan how to implement their decision.

The first time a person does something it is often awkward, whether it is a physical skill, like riding a bike, or a mental one, like speaking a foreign language. In this case, problem solving may be new both to the adult who acts as a coach or facilitator and to the child. Problem solving is easier to start when the child has the required skills, has some experience generating and evaluating alternatives for others, and begins in a low stress situation. In the next chapter we will look at how parents can set the stage for problem solving with toddlers and preschoolers.

CHAPTER 3: SETTING THE STAGE FOR PROBLEM SOLVING WITH PRESCHOOLERS

"Is it really possible for preschoolers to solve problems? Doesn't the process seem too advanced for them?" The answer is, "It depends on the preschooler." Certainly the process outlined in the previous chapter is above the head of very young children, however many children are more capable of grasping the concepts than their parents imagine. The ability of very young children to solve problems is illustrated in the following examples.

I was amazed to see Anna, age 2½, avoid a problem with 2 year old Danny. Anna had been pushing a baby carriage around the room when Danny came up and grabbed the handle to play with it himself. Anna turned to him and said "You get one." Danny took his hand off the bar, but stayed where he was making it difficult for her to move. Anna repeated her request. When he stayed where he was, Anna took his hand and walked with him to where the other carriage was parked.

I would not have believed preschoolers could resolve problems if I had not seen my 15 month old nephew (Ethan) distract my son Paul from the rocking horse. Paul loves to ride rocking horses, so he climbed on Ethan's horse as soon as he saw it. Paul had been riding for a while when Ethan came and asked to ride. Paul continued to rock. Ethan then went and got a very colorful pull toy and slowly pulled it through Paul's line of vision. Paul hopped off the horse to investigate the toy. Ethan immediately got on the horse.

These children are certainly the exception rather than the rule, especially since, in both cases, the parents had not consciously promoted problem solving. However, many children who watch people closely notice different ways people get what they want. There are several things adults working or living with toddlers can do to encourage the development of problem solving skills.

BUILDING SKILLS WITH TODDLERS

Parents of children less than three often want to know what they can do *now* to help their child learn to share. There are four things adults can do to help them collect the information and experiences they will need to solve problems: offer choices, suggest different alternatives, talk about feelings, and observe the consequences of behavior.

Offer choices. Children need to be able to make decisions to negotiate. The simplest way to teach this is to give children lots of experience in decision making. For the 12 month old, you can let him decide which pajamas he wants to wear to sleep. In the beginning, you may need to hold both garments in front of the child and make a guess as to which he prefers. Most children will catch on and point to their choice. With an 18 month old, you might ask if he wants to be carried or walk to bed. When he turns and runs away, you can pick him up and say, "You choose to be carried." As children grow older, the choices can include objects the child cannot see.

Offer different ideas. Children learn to problem solve first by what they experience around them. If they are told only to wait their turn, then that is all they will know. If someone grabs a toy from them, grabbing will be an alternative for them. There are many ways toddlers can get toys—some desirable, some not. For example, a toddler can grab a toy, hit a child then pick up the toy if it is dropped, ask for it, trade for it, or set a timer to take turns. The more options children experience, the more likely they are to get what they want in an acceptable way.

Young children learn most easily when the ideas are divided into small pieces and introduced gradually. For example:

When Beth was little, I decided to help her learn how to share with other children. I began by teaching her how to trade for what she wanted. At first when she wanted a toy, I would give her something I thought the other child would like and tell her to give it to the other child. Usually that would work. Then I began to offer her two toys and ask her which she thought the other child would like. She would choose one and then take it to the other child. Next, I would ask her what she thought the child would like. She would then pick a toy and take it to the other child.

After she got the hang of trading, I showed her how to ask for what she wanted and how to use the timer to take turns. Each time I introduced a new approach, I tried to break the task into small pieces. Now at three, she is very skillful at getting what she wants in appropriate ways.

EXERCISE 3-1: Alternatives for Toddlers (page 37)

Talk about feelings. Many toddlers are aware of the feelings of those around them. They may show this by taking their bottle or blanket to a crying child. You can increase children's awareness of feelings by talking about what you see around you. "Mark is crying because he is hurt," "I feel lonely because Daddy is out of town tonight," or "You look proud."

You can talk about how different people act when they have the same feeling. For example, Aunt Emily cries when she is happy, but Mommy cries when she is sad or mad. Children can learn the variety of feelings the same way they learn the hues of color—simple repetition in different situations. As children begin to have labels for feelings, they can relate them to events.

People often feel the way they do because of the events that happen to them. A toddler can learn that "It hurt Jenny when you hit her," or "Sarah is mad because Brad took her book away." They can also learn what helps others feel better: "You helped Danny feel better by giving him a book. I'm proud of you."

Observe consequences of different behaviors. A toddler can learn about different options by observing them in action. Some children do this by themselves. Other children need to have the options pointed out to them. Comment on both acceptable and unacceptable alternatives and explain what is wrong with the unacceptable ideas. This is illustrated in the following examples.

Megan was sitting on her mother's lap watching some other children at preschool. Mom remarked, "Jessica looks like she wants the puppet Brad is looking at. I wonder what she will do?" Jessica grabbed the puppet and started to play with it herself. Brad began to cry. "Jessica took Brad's puppet. Brad is mad that Jessica took his puppet. Now look what's happening. Teacher took the puppet from Jessica and gave it back to Brad."

EXERCISE 3-1: Alternatives for Toddlers

Instructions: Look at each situation below and decide three things the adult could do to help the toddler get what he or she wants.

1. Jenny wants the book that Aaron is looking at. She came to Mom and "asked" for help.

   a. _____.

   b. _____.

   c. _____.

2. Matt wants to ride the scooter that Erin is riding. You look up and Matt is trying to push Erin off the scooter.

   a. _____.

   b. _____.

   c. _____.

3. Jason wants to put clothes pins in the same bottle Sarah is. Sarah does not want help and is beginning to scream.

   a. _____.

   b. _____.

   c. _____.

Possible answers

1: a. Tell Jenny to ask Aaron for the book.
   b. Read the book to both Aaron and Jenny.
   c. Give Jenny a book to offer Aaron.

2: a. Give Matt a special toy to trade for.
   b. Ask Erin if both Matt and Erin could ride together.
   c. Interest him in something else until Erin is done.

3: a. Give Jason a container and small blocks to put in it.
   b. Show Jason and Sarah how to alternate putting clothes pins in the bottle.
   c. Set a timer so they can take turns.

Dad and Andy are sitting with the children while they build blocks. Dad remarks to Andy, "Will is watching Robin play with an ambulance. He looks like he wants to play with it. He just offered Robin a dump truck. She is trading. Now he can use the ambulance."

Grownups can also call a child's attention to different ways children get what they want. They grab, wait, ask or trade. Sometimes one way is successuful, sometimes it is not. When discussing consequences, adults need to point out for children both "good" actions and "bad."

PROBLEM SOLVING WITH THREE TO FIVE YEAR OLDS

Most three and four year olds can learn to negotiate. To teach these children, adults need to determine what prerequisite skills and what experience in making decisions the child has, then introduce the problem solving concept and provide the opportunity to practice.

Assessing Skills Needed For Problem Solving

A preschooler's ability to solve social problems is dependent, in part, on his or her cognitive understanding of the skills needed. Three skills children need in order to be able to negotiate are: (1) the ability to listen and pay attention to others, (2) an understanding of certain language concepts and (3) the ability to recognize and understand certain feeling concepts. These skills are described more fully in the previous chapter.

These abilities are present in some children as early as three and in most children by age seven. If an adult pushes children to negotiate before they have the needed skills, it is usually frustrating for both adult and child. A series of "assessment games" is provided in Appendix A. The purpose of these "assessment games" is to help adults identify skills children need to learn before they can problem solve with someone else.

Introduce The Problem Solving Process

When children have the needed skills and some experience making decisions, they are ready to begin solving problems themselves. The process can be introduced by modeling appropriate behavior, and reading books that illustrate looking for alternatives *before* acting.

Modeling problem solving. This is usually the most effective way to introduce the process. Modeling involves *both* using the process to solve problems and explaining what you are doing. The modeling can be with another adult, an older child, or the child himself.

Reading books. Stories of all kinds can be used to introduce the concepts of problem solving. The Children's Problem Solving Series mentioned in the previous chapter illustrates the problem solving process directly. Other books can be used if the adult helps the child identify the problem, the alternatives, and the consequences of those alternatives. Sometimes it is useful to mention that a character has problems because he or she did not look at the possible consequences before acting.

Provide Opportunity for Practice

Preschool children learn best when given many opportunities to practice. The more "real" the activity, the easier it is for the young child to understand. For this reason, using puppets to practice thinking of new ideas will probably work better than discussing a conflict that occurred earlier that day or another day.

Puppet plays. Many children love making puppet shows. They particularly like having an audience. The children can use a script or make the play as they go. The scripts for the 'puppet show' can come from the children's experiences or can be adapted from the dialogs in Appendix C.

Make-believe. Children who enjoy make-believe and imaginary play can practice problem solving in their play. Again, adults can develop situations from the child's experience or from the dialogs in this book. One way adults can approach make-believe is to set up a situation and have the children act out many different ways for the story to resolve itself. Some parents find it useful to take part in the activities while others find it works more smoothly if they are an audience.

Interestingly, research has found that when young children take different parts in plays, it increases their ability to see a situation from another person's perspective. With this in mind, encourage the children to take a variety of roles in their play.

Telling stories. Many preschoolers like to make up stories. You can encourage this by asking the child to tell you a story about a child who had a problem. For example, "Tell me a story about a little girl who wanted the toy someone else had and the different ways she tried to get it." An added incentive for some children is to tape record the story and then play it back. If the child does not usually make up stories, you can model making up stories and playing them back.

Teaching someone to problem solve. One of the best ways to learn material is to teach it. This is true with preschool children as well as older children. A four year old can show a toddler different ways to "share." You may wish to explain to the preschooler that younger childen need to be shown many times, so he does not get frustrated when the toddler does not learn quickly.

Preschool children can and do learn to solve social conflicts. As with older children, their ability to negotiate increases with their ability to understand feelings, to generate alternatives and to predict possible consequences of those ideas. Toddlers' and preschoolers' interests and abilities are focused on situations that are concrete and real to them. Introducing ideas and practicing problem solving is most effective when it relates directly to what the child has experienced personally, or through observation or stories. During the preschool years, adults often need to encourage children to negotiate. Some specific ways to encourage problem solving are presented in Chapter 6. As children grow older they can begin to negotiate on their own. In the next chapter we will look at how children can use this step-by-step process to solve problems themselves.

1. Stop
2. Identify
3. Generate
4. Evaluate
5. Plan

CHAPTER 4: PROBLEM SOLVING WITH SCHOOL AGED CHILDREN

Up to this point we have focused on how parents can intervene to help children negotiate their conflicts. When adults intervene they take responsibility for calming things down and for helping the children follow the steps. Older children can be taught to apply the problem solving process without assistance. In this chapter we will look at the steps children need to use to solve their problems, and some ways to encourage them to use this process. Athough this section is written for adults, the language is directed towards children. You may invite school aged children to read this chapter if you think it is appropriate for them.

THE SIGEP APPROACH

The ability to solve social problems effectively involves some specific skills. The problem solving process is summarized by the term SIGEP. This term was used by Dr. Eric Trupin. Each letter stands for a particular step: Stop, Identify, Generate, Evaluate, and Plan. You will notice that this is very similar to the intervention process we outlined in the previous chapter. These steps are summarized briefly below.

1. Stop. This first step in problem solving is to stop and think. Later in this chapter we will look at some techniques to help people remain (or become) calm.

2. Identify. The next step is to identify what you are upset about or why you have a problem. Think in terms of specific actions rather than labels or general statements. For example: "He is mean" is a label. "He called me a bad name" is a specific action. It is also helpful to look at the situation from the other person's point of view to see what they need and want.

3. Generate. Think of all the ways you can to solve the problem. Include some impractical or crazy ideas as it helps the creative process and lightens up the session. Postpone evaluating ideas until the next step.

4. Evaluate. Now is the time to evaluate the alternatives. What will happen with each of the ideas? How practical are they to implement? When you are through evaluating choose an idea. (Remember that you can come back and choose again if that choice does not work.)

5. Plan. The last step is planning how to implement your idea. What do you do first? Do you need someone's permission or assistance? What is the best way to carry the idea through? Good decisions sometimes fail because no further thought was given about implementing the decision.

This process can be used for all types of problems: social conflicts and "physical" problems. Social conflicts may develop with people at home, at school, or at the playground. Problems may also occur with "things" in the physical world like a bicycle that keeps falling down or scissors that do not work smoothly.

Next we will look at each of these steps in more detail.

ONE:
STOP &
KEEP CALM

Staying calm is a great plan, and sometimes very difficult. Two aspects to follow are: (1) how do you know you are getting mad (or have a problem), and (2) ways to keep calm (or relax if you are already upset).

How do you know you know you have a problem? Problems don't appear full grown. They develop with several steps. The trick to staying calm is to notice some early signs. We will look at several ways people can tell they have a problem.

"He hit me" or *"The police are here."* Most people know they have a problem when someone interferes with what they want. It can be as simple as someone saying "no," or as serious as being hit or finding a police officer at the door. In most cases there is something you did that contributed to the problem. Looking at the reasons becomes step two.

"I want to hit him." Some people know that they have a problem when they want to hurt someone. Again there are steps that lead up to that.

"I feel mad." Some people are good at noticing their feelings. They know they have a problem when they are angry, frustrated or disappointed. Each person's body has its own way of signaling that there is a problem. Some common signals are: tightness or a lump in the stomach or throat, breathing faster, feeling confused, palms getting sweaty, or fists getting tight.

"I think he is getting upset." Some people can guess that trouble is coming by how someone else is feeling. They notice the other person is having trouble talking, his hands or lips are clenched, or that he is somehow "acting" upset.

How to stay calm. There are several ways to keep calm or become calm if you are upset: count to ten, take three breaths, let your anger drain out, or pretend you have a protective shield. You may have some other ways that work for you. These approaches are described below.

Count to ten. One way to calm down is to count to ten, or twenty five if you need to. Counting gives your mind something constructive to do. You can count out loud or in your mind—whatever works for you.

Take three deep breaths. Breathing deeply is a relaxation technique used by people all over the world. Sit or stand as tall as you can and breathe in as deeply as you can. Feel the air making your chest or abdomen large. When you can't breath in anymore, let the air out slowly.

Let anger drain out. When people get angry they often unknowingly tense their muscles -- I unconsciously close my fists. To let the anger drain out, sit or stand comfortably with your feet flat on the floor. Let all your muscles go limp, shake your arms and legs briefly to reduce tension. Then visualize the angry feeling slowly draining out your feet.

Pretend you have a protective shield. When someone else is mad at you they generate a certain amount of energy. It is easy to pick up that energy and be mad too. To avoid picking up the energy, visualize a protective shield. The shield can be like an umbrella that protects you from the rain or like the feathers on a duck that repel the water droplets. The shield can be like the ones in science fiction stories or whatever you need. When you have visualized the shield, you can be calm and let the other person's anger pass you by.

Develop your own specialty. Practice the techniques above or others that work for you. If you remember times you have calmed yourself down, you can get an idea of personal techniques. Jot them down so you can use them when you need them. Experiment with different ways to calm down. Once you are calm you are ready to identify the problem.

TWO:
IDENTIFY
THE
PROBLEM

It is easier to solve a problem if you have a clear understanding of what the problem is. This is done by gathering data, and deciding what your own and other people's needs are.

Questions to ask. The following is a list of questions that may help you identify the problem.

What was happening before the problem? Sometimes looking at what happened before the problem helps you to understand the problem itself. Was this the first time something like this happened? Who was involved?

How do I feel? Scared, angry, frustrated, ignored, helpless? Understanding your feelings often helps give an idea of what you want.

What do I want? Someone to behave differently than they are? More money? People to leave me alone? Someone to be friends with?

What do other people involved in the situation want? Do they want something I have? Revenge for something they think I did? Time to be with me? Time to be alone?

Who else is this a problem for? Does someone else have this problem too?

Define the problem. To define the problem, focus on the specific *behavior* that is difficult for you. Avoid general terms. For example, "He is mean" might become "He knocked my books into the mud puddle"; or "She is a jerk" might become "She laughs at me whenever I try to talk to her." The description should be clear enough that someone else could identify the problem from it.

You can define the problem by describing what is happening that you don't like, or what you would like to have happen that is not. In defining what you want, it is helpful to distinguish between "needs" and "wants." When I am hungry I may say, "I am so hungry I need a whole steak," but that is really a want. What I *need* is food. There are many kinds of food that will stop the hunger.

THREE:
GENERATE
IDEAS

When you list ideas, let your imagination run free. List both practical and impractical ideas. Include at least three really crazy ideas. When your mind is free enough to think of crazy ideas it is free enough to think of new practical ideas.

List all ideas. Write down all the ideas you think of—practical and impractical. Often a silly idea will spark a good idea later.

Where to get ideas. There are several ways to get ideas. One way is to list things you aready know. That is what people often do when they write down ideas. Second, alter or change those ideas in some way—make them simpler, more complicated, more fun. Third, write ideas that are totally wild. Four, look at how other people handle similar problems and adapt those ways. Another way to get ideas is to pretend you are from outer space and can use solutions that are not available to earthlings, then describe what they might be like. You can also imagine you are very rich or very poor and think of how you would handle the problem then.

Questions to start ideas. The following are some specific questions you can ask:

"How can I change the physical setting?" What can you add? What can you remove? What can you rearrange to make the situation better. For example, "If people want the music quieter, I could use ear phones."

"Who could help me?" Could a friend, parent or sibling assist you in getting what you want? For example, "You got up late and still need to pack your lunch. Maybe your brother could make it while you get dressed?"

"Can I do things in a different order?" Would it help to start earlier, later or rearrange the order? "I want to go skiing tomorrow instead of doing my Saturday job. I could do my job tonight."

"How can I prevent the problem from happening again?" Could you have avoided the problem if you planned your time better, watched where you were going, or listened to what people said to you? For example, "I would not have gotten paint on my shirt if I had listened to Dad when he said, 'Watch out for the wet paint in the hall.'"

"Can I buy (or trade) for help or assistance?" Who might help you or fix this problem for you if you offered services in return. For example, "I want to go camping with the scouts next weekend, but I am responsible for the dog. Maybe my sister will trade and do it next week if I do it this week."

Do not evaluate ideas. The process of evaluation stops the creative flow of ideas. You will evaluate ideas next. Let your imagination rule now.

FOUR: EVALUATION

Now is the time to evaluate. Consider what will happen with these ideas and how practical they are to implement. Discard ideas with a low chance of success, and those that are too costly in terms of time, money or personal energy.

Look at the consequences. What will happen if you implement an idea? Will it get what you want? What problems will it have? How will it affect other people?

Look at the process of implementation. How much will it cost? How long will it take? Do you have enough energy to follow through with that idea? Who else is needed to support the idea?

Choose a plan. Choose the idea that best meets your need. Keep the list of ideas so that if this doesn't work, you have a head start next time.

FIVE: THE PLAN

The final step is planning and implementing the idea you choose. If you have considered what is involved in the evaluation stage, planning should be relatively easy.

Plan the steps involved. What do you need to do first? Do you need someone's permission or support? If so, how can you best get it?

Decide on a time to evaluate the idea. Did this plan work or do you need to try again? If it didn't work, what went wrong? If it did work, remember that too.

Implement the plan. This is sometimes the hardest part. Carry out your idea. Remember, if it works, great; if not, you can find another one.

Congratulate yourself on a job well done. If you have been successful, make a note of what worked. If it was not sucessful, look at the ideas you generated and try something else.

The following is an example of how one child used the SIGEP process to resolve a difficulty with his sister. You can notice how he went through the five steps.

EXAMPLE OF SIGEP IN ACTION

Ricky (age 11) had gone out to eat at a nice resturant with his parents, grandparents and sister, Becky (age 7). Ricky and his mom were sitting side by side talking as they waited for a table to become available. Suddenly, Becky got up, came over and sat down between her brother and mother, forcing them apart. Ricky was very quiet for a moment or two and then got up and moved to the other side. Mom was so impressed by his effective behavior she asked him how he decided to do that. This was his response:

"When Becky pushed her way in, I felt real mad. (Stop) I knew I was mad because I made a fist and wanted to bop her one. (Identify) I decided I was mad because I wanted to sit next to mom and she butted in. (Generate) At first I thought of hitting her or pushing her off on the floor. I could ask her to move, try to negotiate or move myself. (Evaluate) Finally I decided to move myself, because if I hit her or asked her to move, she would make a big scene and I would be embarrased. I didn't ask her to make a deal because if she wanted to make a deal she wouldn't have butted in in the first place. (Plan) So I just moved. It worked, but she shouldn't have butted in."

If you wish to practice identifying the SIGEP steps you can do the following exercise.

EXERCISE 4-1: Recognizing the SIGEP Steps. (page 45)

The SIGEP approach is an effective way to deal with problems, whether the problems are with people or "things." The process is the same: Stop, Identify, Generate, Evaluate, and Plan. One benefit of the approach is that it can be used alone or with other people. When people can use this process, they are ready to take control of events. In the next chapter we will look at some ways to encourage children to negotiate with one another.

EXERCISE 4-1: Recognizing the SIGEP steps.

Instructions: Read the description below and notice how Eric used the SIGEP process to decide how to respond when his sister poked him. Write the name of the following steps beside the paragraph that describes it:

    A. Stop and calm down
    B. Identify the problem
    C. Generate ideas
    D. Evaluate ideas
    E. Plan (and decide)

"The SIGEP steps can keep you out of trouble. For example, yesterday I was about to bop my sister Annie when I remembered the SIGEP steps.

Annie had a bunch of toothpicks and I was curious what she was doing with them, so I went over and looked. I was just standing there near her and she pokes me with a sharp toothpick.

(1) I didn't think demanding an apology would work. If she poked me, she probably wanted to make me mad, and she would say "No!" and make me mad more. Ignoring her might be a good idea but I wanted her in trouble too.

(2) I want to get even without getting in trouble.

(3) I let some of the angry feeling drain out and then looked at why I was angry. I was mad because she hurt me, I wanted to hurt her back.

(4) None of the ideas were really good, but I knew I would get in big trouble if I hurt her, so I complained to Mom."

(5) When she poked me I got mad. I knew I was mad because my muscles were all tight, and my foot was moving towards her. As soon as I knew I was mad, I put on the brakes and came to a screeching halt.

(6) Several ideas flashed in my mind. I could kick her, punch her or hit her. I didn't think I could get away with that since Mom was in the room. I also thought I could tell Mom, ignore her or demand an apology.

Answer:

A. Stop and calm down: 5 & 3
B. Identify the problem: 2

C. Generate ideas: 6
D. Evaluate ideas: 1
E. Plan and decide: 4

CHAPTER 5: HOW TO USE NEGOTIATION TO RESOLVE CHILD-PARENT CONFLICTS

So far we have concentrated on child-child conflicts. We have seen ways parents can help young children to find solutions that are agreeable to everyone, and we have seen how older children can negotiate without adult assistance. This same process can be used to help children and parents resolve their conflicts.

PARENTS'
OPTIONS

Before I introduce how negotiation can be modified to work for child-parent conflicts, I will review the other options available to parents. Parents can ignore the offending behavior, restructure the environment, direct the child's behavior, offer the child choices, or negotiate with the child. Each option is appropriate in some situations and not in others.

Ignoring requires not responding to the conflict situation. It is appropriate when a child misbehaves simply to get attention. It is also appropriate if the parent does not have the time or energy to enforce another approach. (However, if you continue to ignore a situation that is important to you, you do both yourself and the child a disservice.)

Restructuring the environment to eliminate the problem involves adding, removing, or changing things to increase the chances of getting what you want. For example, one parent chained her scissors to her desk so her children could not remove them.

Structuring the environment can be done by the parent alone or as the result of negotiation with the children. Structuring is appropriate when the situation lends itself to rearrangement and when no one else's needs are infringed upon.

Directing children's behavior tells them what you expect them to do. To be effective it must be specific. For example, "Stop bugging me" is vague, while "I want to finish reading this chapter, play by yourself until I am done" is clear. Directing can be accompanied with choices which provide the child with several ways to accomplish the direction.

Directing behavior is appropriate when action is needed immediately. For example, you may wish to direct behavior when you are being hurt, something is being damaged, or your patience is wearing thin. Again, if you frequently find your patience wearing thin, if you are often tired or don't have time, look and see how you can modify your activities to provide more time and less stress.

Sometimes children need limits and are unable to set them for themselves. When this happens, it is appropriate for parents to set the limits by directing their behavior. For example, Mary (age 8) had a lot of trouble getting her Saturday jobs done. The jobs were very simple and could easily be done by her in ten minutes. However, she would ask for extensions, trade jobs with her siblings and "forget" to do the jobs. Finally, Mom kindly but firmly told her that she must do them and, further, they needed to be done by noon on Saturday. In this case, the struggle was over. Mary switched her energy from trying to get out of doing the jobs to trying to do them quickly.

Offering choices involves presenting children with several alternatives and letting them decide what to do. The choices offered can be between possibilites the child finds desirable, or between a behavior the parent desires and the consequence if it is not done. An example of the latter is: "You may finish your meal and have what you want for a bedtime snack, or you can be excused from the table now and eat the rest of your dinner for bedtime snack."

Offering choices is appropriate when there are several possibilities, when you have time for the child to decide, and when the child is capable of deciding. There are times when even school aged children are too tired, hungry, sick, or upset to make responsible decisions.

Negotiation involves children in identifying the problem and finding a solution that works for both child and parent. Later in this chapter, two ways parents and children can resolve conflict will be discussed in detail.

Negotiation is appropriate when both parent and children have the time, energy, and experience needed to negotiate. In conflict situations that repeat again and again, parents can schedule a time for negotiation if the moment of conflict is not suitable.

Problem solving is useful with children of all ages. Children are more likely to comply with a decision they helped make than a decision presented to them. Negotiation is particularly valuable as children grow older, and the parent's method of guidance needs to shift from relying primarily on power (either physical, psychological or personal) to relying on influence and consensus. This shift is necessary because as children grow in size and independence, parents can no longer enforce rules as they once did. For example, if a toddler refuses to come in, an adult can easily pick him up and and carry him in. The squirming will make it more difficult but not impossible. As the child becomes a teen, it is no longer possible to carry him if he resists.

In some situations, several options are possible. The following example illustrates how the various approaches might work for a specific situation.

Paul and his daughter were out hiking on an overgrown trail. Becky was walking directly in front of her dad and occasionally let a branch snap back and hit him.

Ignoring: Paul could continue to walk right behind Becky without commenting that the branches were hitting him.

Structuring the environment: Paul could walk in front of Becky. That way she could not accidentally hit him with a branch.

Direct: Dad could tell Becky to watch how she went through branches because it hurt him when they snapped back.

Offer choices: Paul could offer her the choice of walking in back or holding the branches so they didn't hit him.

Negotiate: Dad could say, "Becky, we seem to have a problem. You like to walk freely along the trail, and I don't like to be hurt by branches snapping at me. What can we do so we both can be happy?"

In the following exercise, you can list various ways a problem can be solved.

EXERCISE 5-1: Looking for Options (page 49)

EXERCISE 5-1: Looking at Options in Child-Parent Conflicts

INSTRUCTIONS: Read the following situation and decide how you could ignore, restructure the environment, direct behavior, offer choices, and negotiate with a child. Remember, not all ideas need to be reasonable.

Situation:
Last week and the week and the week before, Jason (age 10) took off on his bike Saturday morning before doing his jobs. Jason's family has the rule that Saturday jobs must be done before people can leave the house. He does do the jobs when he returns, but his sisters do not think it is fair for him to go riding while they do their jobs.

1. Ignore: _____

   _____

   How effective would this be? _____

2. Restructure the environment: _____

   _____

   How effective would this be? _____

3. Direct behavior: _____

   _____

   How effective would this be? _____

4. Offer Jason choices: _____

   _____

   How effective would this be? _____

5. Negotiate with Jason: _____

   _____

   How effective would this be? _____

Possible responses:

1. *Ignore the behavior:*
   Description — Do nothing. Focus on the idea that he is doing his jobs.
   Effectiveness — Ignoring would probably have no effect on Jason's behavior.

2. *Structure the environment:*
   Description — Padlock Jason's bike and leave a note saying it will be opened as soon as the jobs are done.
   Effectiveness — Jason would probably get mad and act uncooperatively if he found his bike locked.

3. *Direct the situation:*
   Description — Remind him of the family rule. "Jason, vacuum the rugs and take out the trash before you go riding today."
   Effectiveness — It might work or might not, depending on Jason's mood at the time.

4. *Offer choices:*
   Description — "Jason, the family rule is 'Do your jobs before you go out.' You may do your jobs before you go biking or lose the privilege of going biking."
   Effectiveness — It might work.

5. *Negotiate with the child:*
   Description — "Jason, we have a problem. The family rule says family members will do their jobs before they go out. For the last two weeks, you went out before you did your job. What do you see is the problem?"
   Effectiveness — It would probably work.

Each of the five approaches described above could be discussed much more extensively. However, since the focus of this book is cooperation, we will concentrate on how adults can negotiate with children. Several books which offer other alternatives for parent-child conflicts are listed in Appendix D.

TWO LEVELS OF PROBLEM SOLVING

When conflicts arise between parents and children, parents may choose to work it out with the children. If parents wish to involve a child in solving the problem, they need to consider the child's problem solving ability. The beginning level looks for one idea that will work for both parent and child. This process is called "A Better Way." After children gain experience finding one solution, they can begin to look for several ways to solve the problem.

BEGINNING LEVEL: "A Better Way"

The easiest way to begin negotiation is by hunting for "A Better Way." Children do not need to have experience in problem solving to find a better way. However, they need to be able to talk, listen, and make decisions. This generally happens about age three. The adult begins by describing what the child wants, follows with what the parent or other person wants, and finishes with a suggestion of something that the adult thinks will work for both of them. When children understand the process, ask them to suggest "A Better Way." The three steps are summarized in the phrase, "Your way, my way and a better way." This process can be seen in the following example.

Beth (age 3½) had lots of experience in problem solving. Normally, she was very agreeable; however, this morning she wanted to take a bath after breakfast. Mom was normally flexible, also; but this morning she wanted to give Beth a bath before breakfast. After reviewing her options, Mom decided to try to find "A Better Way" with Beth.

Mom: Your way is that I give you a bath after breakfast. My way is that I give you a bath now. What is a better way?

Beth: Karl do it now. (Karl was her nine year old brother.)

Mom: Karl, will you give Beth her bath now?

Karl: What do I have to do?

Mom: Beth, what does Karl have to do?

Beth: Get the water.

Mom: Are you willing to run bath water?

Karl: Yes.

Mom: Okay, kids, let's go.

When parents begin to use "A Better Way" they need to be aware of two concerns.

First, they need to check that the "Better Way" is really acceptable to the child. Many young children will agree to an idea suggested by a parent that they don't like. If the child's expression or tone looks like he or she does not like the idea, check it out. One might say, "I heard you say you would take a nap now, but you look like you don't like the idea. Remember, a better way is one we both like. Is the idea really okay?"

Second, parents may need to supply the "Better Way." This is especially true for children beginning to negotiate. Before you suggest ideas, try to find out what is behind their desire, and look for ways to meet that desire. One three year old who demanded two cookies accepted two half cookies. He wanted one for each hand. As children begin to suggest ideas, parents are sometimes surprised at what they will suggest. It seems as though children are often satisfied simply to have some say in the result. This is illustrated below.

Jonathan was a very bright seven year old. He had been able to tell time since he was five. One evening he came in to Dad just before his bedtime and said, "Dad, I want to stay up late tonight." Dad had plans for the evening and did not like the idea of spending an hour or two putting an unwilling child to bed.

Dad: Your way is for you go to bed late. My way is for you go to bed now. What is a better way?

Jonathan: (Jonathan thought a moment then replied.)
I will go to bed in five minutes.

Dad: That is fine, but how will you know when the five minutes are up?

Jonathan: I will set the kitchen timer and show you it is right.

Dad: That sounds good to me.

Jonathan set the timer and showed it to his Dad. When it rang, he went to bed with no hassle.

In both of these examples, the first suggestion was acceptable to both parent and child. That is not always the case. When the child's first suggestion is unacceptable, explain why and then suggest the closest idea you can that is acceptable to you. Remember, if your suggestion was unacceptable, find out why and try again. If the child appears to be uncooperative, you can remind him, "If we can't find something that works for both of us, I will decide myself." If negotiation does not work you can fall back on the other four approaches.

As children grow, their ability to generate and evaluate ideas increases, and you can move from finding one idea to finding several ideas and evaluating them for the best solution.

ADVANCED LEVEL: "SIGEP" for Adults and Children

The process parents use to negotiate with children is basically the same as the process children use with children. In this case, however, the parent plays two roles: that of facilitator and that of participant. Because of their double role, effective parents make a special effort to be aware of the child's concern and to avoid using the position of facilitator to the child's disadvantage. In this section, we will look at the five SIGEP steps discussed previously and how they can be adapted for child-parent conflicts.

Stop

Stop. When adults find themselves being drawn into a conflict with children, the first step is to stop and decide how they want to handle the conflict. They can use any of the five options. If the adult decides to problem solve with a child, they both need to calm down enough to negotiate. Several examples of how this can be done are listed below:

1. Matthew (age 10), we appear to disagree about whether or not you can go biking on busy streets. Let's sit down and come to an agreement.

2. You promised to clean the living room before I got back. I am so mad to find the house in a worse mess than when I left, that I am going to my room for a minute and calm down before we talk about this.

3. I can see you are very angry that we are scheduled to go to Grandma's on the same weekend your scout troop is going camping. When you are calm we can see if this problem can be resolved.

Many people find it helpful to remember that anger, in itself, is neither good or bad; however, it can be used appropriately and inappropriately. It is appropriate to be angry when someone has hurt you or treated you disrespectfully. That anger can let the person know how you feel. However it is not appropriate to express your anger in a way that is degrading or hurtful to another person—even if that person caused your hurt. You can use anger constructively by focusing on the behaviors rather than the personality of the other person. For example, "You are just a good-for-nothing slob" can be changed to "I am extremely upset to find the house messier than when I left."

The techniques suggested for how to calm oneself, provided in the chapter on problem solving for school aged children, work for adults as well. You may wish to experiment and see what works best for you. When both parties are calm you can identify the problem. If the problem is simple you may be able to keep the information in your head. If the discussion is lengthy or complex, a pencil and paper will be useful to record the problem, the ideas you generate, notes on evaluation, your final decision, and plans for implementing your decision.

Identify

Identify the Problem. Sometimes identifying the problem is straightforward, other times it is not. When you state the concern, do so in terms of "needs" rather than "solutions." A need is the underlying concern. A solution is one way that the underlying need can be met. For example, the solution stated "I need you to *keep* the living room clean" could be changed to "I want the living room neat *when I come home* at night." When you state a problem in terms of needs, rather than solutions, you increase the possible ways to get what you want. You also increase the chance of finding something that works well for both of you.

When you state the problem, be sure to get the child's agreement that it is the problem. Sometimes it is necessary to look at things from a child's perspective to correctly identify the problem. This can be seen in the example below.

Dad was getting very frustrated. He had asked David to take the trash out three times, and David was still lying on his bed reading a book. Dad was considering doing something rash—like grabbing the book away, or saying something unkind about "lazy" kids. He decided instead to check that his perception—that David was trying to get out of his job—was correct. What he found was that David was planning to empty the trash later. He was trying to finish reading a book he was going to write a report on in school the next day. Dad found that in this case the problem was not one of unwillingness to do the job but one of timing.

When you have both agreed on what the problem is, you are ready to move on to generating ideas.

Generate Ideas

Generate Ideas. The more ideas you have, the more likely you are to find one that you both agree on. Try to come up with at least 20 ideas. When you generate ideas, include crazy ideas as well as practical ones. If you get stuck you can return to the the problem and review it, or look at the "idea starters" below. Remember that this is the time to let your imagination run. After you generate the ideas you will evaluate them.

Kids Can Cooperate

Idea starters: Who else can do it? Where else can it be done? What else can we use to do it or solve the problem? When can we do it? How would Superman or Wonder Woman solve the problem? What can we add to make it easier? What can we remove to eliminate the problem?

Generally the adult is responsible for writing down or remembering the ideas. Write ideas in the children's words or use two or three word phrases. If you rewrite the ideas, children may think that their ideas are not good enough.

Evaluate Ideas

Evaluate the ideas. You can begin by reading the list of ideas one by one and checking how people feel about each idea. Put one star in front of each idea for each person who finds the alternative acceptable. As this is done, people will often voice their objections to particular ideas. Jot those objections down, also. If you are lucky you will have several ideas that everyone likes. When that happens, you can proceed to making a decision.

In many cases, however, no idea has everyone's approval. When that happens, consider the ideas with the most supporters and see how they can be modified to be acceptable to the others. In the following example, an idea was developed that required getting outside support.

Ellen (age 6) wanted a kitten intensely. When she and Mom reviewed their alternatives they hit a stalemate. Mom did not want to be responsible for the care and feeding of the cat, and she did not feel Ellen was old enough to be completely responsible herself. They were stuck until Ellen asked her brother, Tom (age 12), if he would help take care of a kitten so they could get one. As it turned out, Tom was delighted to agree since he would also like a cat. Both children agreed that Ellen would feed the kitten twice a day, and Tom would change the litter box twice a week.

As you evaluate the ideas, be sure the child or children really agree to the idea. Children will sometimes accept a solution that they don't like because they want to be nice and helpful, and they do not see any alternatives they really like. As children gain more experience in finding alternatives, they can continue working even though they don't see one they like yet. If you suspect the child might not like a proposed idea, remind him or her that you are committed to finding an idea that works for both of you.

When all the ideas are evaluated and at least one idea is acceptable to all the people involved in the conflict, you are in position to make a decision and implement it.

Plan

Develop a Plan. Many good ideas falter because there was no plan for implemention and evaluation. Differences arise in people's expectations. In the situation above there are many issues that need to be resolved. Some of the issues for owning a kitten are:

Who is responsible for buying food and litter? Who washes the kitty's dish? Who sweeps up litter the kitty kicks out of the box? Where will the kitty sleep? If the kitten vomits or has an "accident," who cleans up the mess? How do we choose a kitten? How much can we spend? Who will check on what shots it needs? And, how soon can we get one?

When you have made a decision, consider how it will be implemented. Consider, also, what could go wrong with the decision. The purpose of this is to allow you to plan in advance how you might handle the situations. Unexpected problems rarely cause major difficulties if there is a structure for dealing with them.

Problem Solving Examples

The following two examples show how parents and children can negotiate. The first is an informal agreement, and the second is a long and involved negotiation.

First example: Dad needed Jason for a while to help hold things that he was gluing together. Normally, Jason (age 10) would be happy to help, but at that time he was involved in putting together a model space ship and didn't want to be interrupted.

Dad: Jason, I need your help.
Jason: Did I say I would help you?
Dad: No, but I need it now.
Jason: Well, what will you give me back?
Dad: What would you like?
Jason: You pitch ball while I practice hitting.
Dad: How long do you want me to help you.
Jason: As long as I help you.
Dad: Okay.
Jason: Can I save it 'till tomorrow?
Dad: Yes.
Jason: Can I save it 'till I want?
Dad: Yes. I will give you a card you can trade in for extra help.

Second example: Eight year old Kari's room was a disaster. The junk averaged six inches deep, and there was nowhere to move without stepping on things. Kari liked her mom to come in and read her a story at night. Mom decided she couldn't stand the mess any longer, and she would see if she and Kari could resolve the problem. Mom decided that the best way to introduce problem solving together was through imaginary "Mary."

Mom: I would like your ideas about a problem with a girl called Mary. Mary's room is a big mess, and her mom thinks it is time to clean it up. First of all, Mary and her mother need to decide what the problem is. Do you think that Mary likes her room messy?
Kari: No.
Mom: If she doesn't like a messy room why is her room messy.
Kari: Because she forgets to put her stuff away.
Mom: So, she actually likes it clean, she just doesn't ... (Mom tries to remember.)
Kari: Try to keep it clean.
Mom: So the problem is, "How to help Mary remember to put her things away?"
Kari: Yes.
Mom: Okay. What I would like us to do now is figure out ideas for Mary. Ideas that might help her. Good ideas and crazy ideas. So what is one idea for Mary?
Kari: That she cleans it up herself or that she asks her mother.

Mom: What else could she do? (No response.) What are some crazy ideas?

Kari: They could fall over each other picking up things.

Mom: How about if they put elastic bands on things so they snap back in place? (Kari laughs and Mom continues.) I will review the ideas so far. Mary cleans by herself, she asks her mother to help, they fall over each other putting things away and they put elastic bands on things so they snap back into place. Another idea is that they throw away lots of her stuff so she has more room.

Kari: She throws away clothes she doesn't need.

Mom: What is something more?

Kari: Don't ask me.

Mom: They could put more shelves in her room. Okay, what do you think might happen if Mary did not keep her room clean?

Kari: At night her parents might come in and throw some of her stuff away.

Mom: Another idea is: hire a housekeeper to clean the room. What is something else she can do? (Pause.) Divide the room in half. She can have one half clean and the other half messy.

Kari: Yeah.

Mom: (Counts the ideas.) We have ten ideas. We need five more. What is another one?

Kari: Don't - ask - me - any - more!

Mom: Oh, but you have good ideas. How about some more crazy ideas?

Kari: No.

Mom: Okay, I have one — how about training the pussy cat to clean the room?

Kari: Yeah. (Giggle.) And train a dog to clean up.

Mom: Or building a robot to clean up. Okay, let's change the approach. What do you think would help Mary keep her room clean?

Kari: Build a robot.

Mom: What would make her want to keep her room clean?

Kari: (Repeats questioningly.) What would make Mary want to keep her room clean?

Mom: Yes, like would it help if she was given something when it was clean, if it rained in her room at night when the room was messy, or if it was messy she couldn't watch TV? What sorts of things would make her want to keep her room clean?

Kari: Watch extra TV when it is clean.

Mom: Is there something that Mary's Mom could give her, or do for her, to help her remember to put things away?

Kari: Stickers.

Mom: Well, lets look at all the ideas and see what we have. (She reads the list.) As I read the list this time, tell me how you like the idea, and I will mark your answer on the list. (Mom reads the list and records Kari's responses.) There are a lot of ideas that you like. Which of the ideas do you think will work best?

Kari: Robot and hire a housekeeper.

Mom: Okay, now what ideas do you think will help Mary remember to put her things away?

Kari: Get TV time or stickers when her room is clean.

Mom: How about if she gets a ticket each time her room is clean and when she has five tickets she can get a sticker?

Kari: NO! (Pause.) I have an idea. (Excited.) Remember the prize box? You give me tickets when my room is clean, and I can save them up and get things from the prize box.

Mom: That is okay with me. The plan is to put stickers and TV time cards in the prize box. And then write prices on things in the prize box. When your room is clean I will give you tickets. You can save the tickets to get things you want from the prize box. For example, a sticker might be worth five tickets. Would that be okay?

Kari: Yes.

Mom: Next question: How often and when should you get tickets—once a day, once an hour, when you come and ask for an inspection?

Kari: When I ask for an inspection.

Mom: When should we check to see how this plan is working—one week or two?

Kari: One.

Mom: If your room is neater, we can continue with the tickets. If not, we will need to look for another idea.

Ideas list

Problem: How can Mary remember to put away her things?

Mary cleans up herself — no
Ask Mom for help — yes
Fall over each other cleaning up — no
Put elastic bands on things — no
Throw away extra toys —no
Throw away extra clothes — yes
Put up more shelves —yes
Hire a housekeeper — yes
Divide the room — yes
Train the pussy cat to clean — no
Train a dog to clean — no
Build a robot — yes
Watch extra TV when room is clean — yes
Sticker when room is clean — yes

Kids Can Cooperate

SPECIAL CONCERNS FOR ADULTS

Children negotiate most willingly when they feel as competent as the others participating. For that reason it is important that adults resist the temptation to use their greater experience to manipulate the child.

1. Hunt for win-win solutions. Find solutions that work for both parent and child.

2. Tell children their ideas and feelings are important. Although this is always important in child-adult negotiation, it is particularly true when you are beginning.

3. Resist the temptation to "push" for your ideas. Sometimes parents are tempted to use negotiation as a method to introduce or draw from their children the answer they believe is "right." Children will quickly sense there is a hidden motive and usually decide that the adult is not really trying to negotiate.

4. Suggest some crazy ideas. When people begin to list ideas, they usually list the ones they already knew. One way to stimulate the creative process is to think of silly or wild ideas. When people are free enough to think of crazy ideas, they are free enough to think of new good ideas. If you offer wild ideas, your children will know it is really okay for them to do likewise.

5. Record all ideas. When you decide not to record an idea, you are evaluating it. Evaluation slows the creative process. In addition, children may decide you really don't want crazy ideas and censor their own ideas.

6. Check that the solution chosen is really okay with the child. Look at the child's body language. Listen to his words and tone of voice. Does the child act enthusiastic about the solution? If there is some doubt, ask directly. For example, "I heard you say you were willing to rake the lawn, but I feel as though you really didn't like the idea." Or, "You agreed to cook on Friday. You usually don't like to cook—are you sure it is really okay with you? If it is not, we can find another solution."

7. Involve all people who will be affected by the decision. Sometimes a potential solution involves other people. Include them in your planning. If you know they will be involved before you begin, include them in the whole process.

8. Plan time for evaluation. Sometimes a plan works well; sometimes it doesn't. Plan a time to evaluate so you don't continue with an undesirable plan or let the solution drift away. If the plan does not work, return to your list of ideas or begin again. If the plan is a success, pat yourself on the back.

Additional examples of child-parent negotiations are included in the next chapter. It is important for parents to remember that negotiation is only one way of dealing with child-parent conflicts. If the child does not choose to cooperate, the parent can return to the other options. Ways to motivate unwilling children are also discussed in Chapter 6.

CHAPTER 6: ENCOURAGING PROBLEM SOLVING

Thus far, we have looked at a process for helping children negotiate their differences. However, there is a difference between giving children information and motivating them to use it. In this chapter we will look at ways you can encourage children to use this approach. In particular we will look at general encouragement, family rules, self-esteem and motivating the unwilling child.

GENERAL ENCOURAGE-MENT

People do not change their behavior unless they perceive a benefit. This benefit is something the child wants or needs. It can be as concrete as a sticker or toy, or as elusive as a feeling of calmness due to lack of fighting. In other words, a child does not change a behavior just because she is asked; however she may change to please a parent and gain approval, or to avoid an unpleasant scene. We will look at two forms of encouragement: praise and positive reinforcement.

Praise. Praise tells a child you like what she did. To be most effective, praise must be specific, immediate and honest. To illustrate this idea let's look at two possible responses to the same situation.

Situation: David, a child who usually grabs toys from others, has just offered to trade Mikey a truck for the bus he wanted.

Response 1: "Good boy, David. That is the best job of problem solving I have ever seen."

Response 2: "David, I saw you offer Mike a truck. I am glad you are learning to share."

The first response is both grandiose and general. David may not know what he did that elicited "Good boy," and he probably realizes that it wasn't the "best job" mother has ever seen. When someone exaggerates, it may feel as though what was done was not good enough. In the second situation, David was probably glad she noticed and that she was pleased. When praise is immediate, specific and honest it is easier to accept.

It is interesting to note that you can praise effort as well as success. For example, if a child like David has tried trading and asking for the toy, neither of which worked, Mom could have said, "I see you tried to get the bus two ways. First, you asked; and second, you brought a truck. I am pleased you were thinking."

Praise can be non-verbal as well as verbal. Many parents find a smile or an "OK" hand signal works as well as words do. If you use non-verbal praise, be sure your timing is specific enough that the child knows what he did well. Although many children respond well to praise, for some children it is not enough.

EXERCISE 6-1: Recognizing Effective Praise (page 60)

Exercise 6-1: Recognizing Effective Praise

Instructions: Look at each situation below and decide if the parent's comment is effective praise. If it is not, identify the error and rewrite the statement so it is effective.

1. Two preschoolers are quarrelling over a toy. Mom comes in and says to them, "Yesterday you guys did such a good job of solving your problems, why can't you do it today?"

_____

_____

2. To Danny who just told his mother how he and his sister solved a problem. "Danny, that is fantastic. You did a good job of thinking of ideas. No one else is as good a problem solver as you."

_____

_____

3. Dad watches Mandy and Jenny negotiate who gets to be Mommy and Baby when they play house. Mandy has just left to get her baby toys. Dad remarks "Jenny, I am very pleased to see how you listened to Mandy and worked things out together."

_____

_____

4. Mikey and Matt have just cleaned their room and are trying to decide who uses the new baseball mitt and who uses the old one. As Mother walks through the room she smiles at Matt (who has difficulty cooperating with other children) and says "Good boy."

_____

_____

5. Ricky and his sister Becky were arguing over who gets to sit in the front seat of the car. After much discussion they decide to alternate at every stop. Mom comments, "You two did an excellent job of problem solving. You both hung in and talked until you found something that worked for both of you."

_____

_____

Possible answers:

1. *Ineffective* — the praise was not immediate and was accompanied by a negative statement.
   Effective: (On previous day). "You guys did a great job of solving your problem."
2. *Ineffective* — Grandiose, not honest.
   Effective: "Danny that is fantastic. You did a great job of thinking of ideas. You have really learned how to negotiate well."
3. *Effective* — specific, honest and immediate.
4. *Ineffective* — Not specific. Matt does not know if Mom is pleased he cleaned his room or tried to negotiate with Mikey.
   Effective: "Matt you are gaining skill in negotiation. You stuck with Mike until you found a way to solve your problem."
5. *Effective.* The praise was immediate, specific and honest.

Positive reinforcement. For some children, receiving praise does not provide enough motivation for them to change their behavior. These children need a different reinforcer. The reinforcer can be something tangible or something intangible, like time with a parent. Some tangible reinforcers that often work are stickers, stars, sugarless gum or tickets which can be redeemed for something else.

Three steps are involved in setting up a reinforcement system: (1) Find something the child wants or needs enough to change his or her behavior. This is not always easy. Sometimes the things children want are too expensive. If that is the case, establish tickets the child can redeem for the desired item. (2) Decide clearly what behaviors get rewards. NOTE: make the first steps small; for example, beginning to negotiate. If the child can get a ticket only for successfully completing negotiating, it may seem hopeless to him. When you have decided on the system, explain it to your child. (3) Give the reinforcer immediately when the desired behavior is done. This process is illustrated below.

Anne had introduced the concepts of problem solving to her two children, Kevin (age 10) and Mark (age 6). However, they never used it themselves. They preferred to argue over the issue or come to her for help or attention. She decided to encourage their problem solving by rewarding it. She knew that her children liked colored file cards and decided to offer them as a reward.

Anne got them together one afternoon and said, "I am bothered by all the arguing and quarrelling I hear. I know you can solve your problems together if you try. To help you work together, I will give you each one file card if you try to work out your problem, and five if you succeed in finding something that works for both of you.

To be sure they understood the deal, she asked several questions.

Mom: *Okay, what happens if you both want the swing at the same time and you find a solution that you both like?*

Mark: *We get five cards.*

Mom: *Right, you each get five cards. What happens if you try and don't agree?*

Mark: *We each get one.*

Mom: *Right. What happens if you argue?*

Kevin: *Nothing.*

Mom: *Right. I will carry the cards in my pocket so as soon as you negotiate come and tell me.*

Anne was surprised that the file cards worked for both children since Kevin had an allowance that could keep him in ample file cards if he chose to spend it that way. However, the important thing was that the file cards were something the boys were willing to work for.

Anne was fortunate, she found something that would work on the first try. If the children are not responding, the two most common reasons are that the first step (what the children need to do to get the rewards) is too big, or that the reward is not something the child really wants or needs. If you have difficulty finding something that works, you can ask the child what he would like. Some things that have worked for other people are:

Stickers - Any kind.
"TV tickets" that can be redeemed for additional TV time.
Activity cards - Child can draw an activity to do with the parent.

Points or tickets that can be redeemed for a variety of items which have different "prices"; e.g., stickers, 2 points; gum, 2 points; colored pencil, 10 points.

Candy, sugarless gum, mints, fruit.

Story cards - parent reads story on card or chosen by child.

Money - 5 cents for trying, 25 cents for succeeding.

Stars - when enough are accumulated the family goes out to eat.

Praise and positive reinforcement are two forms of encouragement which help children learn to negotiate. Increasing the self-esteem of children in general makes it easier to resolve social conflicts.

ENCOURAGE SELF-ESTEEM

Children with high self-esteem feel lovable and capable. When children feel lovable and capable it is easier for them to see other people's positions and resolve conflicts.

Experiences that build self-esteem. This book is devoted largely to teaching a process that helps children get what they want and respect the needs of others. When children use this process successfully, it will build their sense of control and capability.

One difficulty that many people have is starting a task that is too large or too complicated. You can help your child become more competent by helping him break a task down into small, easily accomplished steps. When you introduce the problem solving concepts in this book, choose a time when your child will be most likely to understand them.

Messages that build self-esteem. Esteem-building messages tell children they are lovable and capable. These messages come in two forms—"being" messages and "doing" messages.

People, both children and adults, need "being" messages. Being messages tell people you are glad they are alive and that their needs are important. Being messages are unconditional. You don't have to earn them. A person deserves them simply for being alive. For example, "I'm glad you are my son (or daughter)" or "Your needs are important."

Children also need "doing" messages. Doing messages tell children they are responsible and capable. Doing messages report times children acted appropriately or state that you believe they can handle a situation appropriately. For example, "You did a good job of problem solving. You came up with an idea that you both like" or "I hear you guys have a problem. You know the problem solving steps. You can resolve it yourself." Doing messages can also be given for skills the child is learning. For example, "You are beginning to learn problem solving. I saw you stop and decide what to do."

Most people find it easier to give one or the other type of message. Children, however, need both kinds of messages. When children receive only doing messages, they often feel they must be continually performing to be of value. Children who receive only being messages may show inappropriate behavior because they feel their actions are unimportant. Fortunately, it becomes easier to give being and doing messages with practice.

EXERCISE 6-2: Recognizing Esteem-Building Messages (page 63)

Kids Can Cooperate

EXERCISE 6-2: Recognizing Esteem-Building Messages

Instructions: Look at each sentence below and decide if it is an esteem-building message. If it is esteem-building check whether it is a "being"(unearned) message or a "doing"(earned) message.

1. Two preschoolers are quarrelling over a toy. Kari comes to Dad to ask for help.

   _____ I'm glad you came, Kari. Your needs are important.

   _____ Kari, I'm glad you came for help. You thought of one way to get what you want.

   _____ What, you again? Can't you see I'm busyı

2. Matt comes to Mom and says, "Mom, I'm bored. Mike won't play with me."

   _____ Matt, you are a good problem solver. You can think of a way to entertain yourself without Mike.

   _____ Don't bother me now. I have enough problems with dinner.

   _____ I can see you're disappointed. What would you like me to do?

3. Ricky and Becky are quarrelling over who gets the front seat of the car. Mother intervenes with —

   _____ Ricky and Becky, you are both caring, capable people. You can figure a way to sit that meets both of your needs.

   _____ Bicker, bicker, bicker. Can't you guys ever solve anything without fighting?

   _____ Becky, I know you want to sit in the front because it is cooler. Ricky, I know you want to sit in the front because you can see out the window better. Let us find a way to meet both your needs.

4. Mom was in the kitchen getting dinner. Nancy came running in crying, "Johnny hit me. Johnny hit me." Johnny followed Nancy saying, "She took my book and wouldn't give it to me."

   _____ You can find a way to get your book back without hitting Nancy. If you need help you can ask for it.

   _____ Johnny, I am glad you are my boy. Your needs are important.

   _____ Why did she take your book? You must have done something to her.

Possible answers

1: a. effective, being
   b. effective, doing
   c. negative, being
2: a. effective, doing
   b. negative, being
   c. effective, doing

3: a. effective, doing
   b. negative, doing
   c. effective, being
4: a. effective, doing
   b. effective, being
   c. negative. doing

Age-appropriate esteem-building messages. Jean Illsley Clarke, in her book *Self-Esteem: A Family Affair,* outlines messages that children need to hear at different ages. For example, infants 0 - 6 months need "being"messages. Babies 6 to 18 months need to know it is okay to explore and that they will be protected. Children 18 months to 3 years old need to hear that they can think and feel for themselves. Children 3 - 6 years old need to hear that they are powerful and they can ask for what they want "straight" (not deviously). Children 6 - 12 years old need to hear that it is okay to disagree with their friends and they can trust themselves to know what is good for them. Children over 12 years old recycle the previous needs again and need messages for separating and for accepting their sexuality.

Examples of Age-Appropriate Messages

age	general message	specific message
Birth to 6 mo.	Your needs are okay.	(To crying baby.) I'm here now. Are you hungry?
	I'm glad you're a boy/girl.	I'm glad you're my son.
	I like to hold you.	I like to hold you.
6-18 months	You don't have to do "tricks" to get attention.	I enjoy watching you explore your world.
	It's okay to do things and get support.	You can explore the room. I'll be here if you need me.
18-36 months	You can think about what you feel.	You can decide if you want to have a tantrum or not.
	I'm not afraid of your anger.	You are certainly angry. I am here if you need me.
	You can be sure about what you want and feel.	(To child watching others finger-paint.) You can decide if you want to finger-paint or not.
3-6 years	You don't have to act mad, sick or cute to get your needs met.	(To child with big smile.) I'm sorry your head aches and you don't need to act sick to get loving.
	You can express your feelings straight.	You can ask for a hug if you want loving.
	You are powerful.	You can figure out how to get what you want by yourself.
6-12 years	It's okay to disagree.	(To children arguing over which book is best.) You have different opinions and it is okay to disagree.

Kids Can Cooperate

	You can trust your "gut" to know what is right for you.	You know what is right for you. You don't have to throw stones at Mr. Bonn's house because Bobby told you to.
	You don't have to suffer to get your needs met.	You can figure out a way have fun even if Erin won't play with you.
12-18	You can be a sexual person and still have needs.	It is okay to ask for a hug. You can be a teen and still want loving.
	You're welcome to come home again.	(To child leaving on a week-long bike trip.) Have a nice trip and we will be happy to see you when you're back.
	It's okay to know who you are.	(To child trying to decide between biking with a church group and basketball with a school group.) You can decide what you will enjoy most.

FAMILY RULES

Part of a child's sense of competence comes from understanding family rules and knowing the consequences when the rules are broken.

Family rules can support cooperation or they can undermine it. All families have rules, whether they are stated or not. When supportive rules are clearly stated and consistently enforced, things run relatively smoothly. When the rules are unclear, change frequently or are inconsistently enforced, it is hard for children to know what behavior is expected.

Recognizing family rules. Sometimes parents do not know what the rules are. One way they can find out is to ask their children. This is illustrated in the following example.

Mother asked her five year old daughter, Pam, what the rules were in their house. The conversation went like this:

Mom: *What rules do we have in our house?*
Pam: *Huh?*
Mom: *What are you supposed to do in this family?*
Pam: *No stealing. Don't smoke in the house. Be friends.*
Mom: *What do you mean "be friends"?*
Pam: *Don't hit or else you will get into trouble?*
Mom: *What kind of trouble?*
Pam: *I don't know.*
Mom: *What happens sometimes?*
Pam: *Go to your room.*

When Mom asked Pam's 11 year old brother Paul, this was the conversation:

Mom: What rules do we have in our house?
Paul: Don't hit.
Mom: What happens if you hit?
Paul: You get in trouble at the whim of the parent.
Mom: What is the whim of the parent?
Paul: In the worst case you might get spanked. On the other end, if the other person was bad too, it might be ignored.
Mom: What usually happens?
Paul: You get sent to your room.

This situation was interesting because both children knew they should not hurt people but the consequence was variable, and Mom was not aware that she was inconsistent.

Rules differ in different families. There are no right or wrong rules. Family rules generally reflect the values of the parents. One parent may value "cooperation" or "sharing," while another parent may value "taking care of number one" or being successful. Each family develops its own set of values, and rules that support those values.

Values can conflict with one another. For example, if the parents value both "cooperation" and "taking care of number one," there will be conflict when suddenly the older daughter has the chance to earn some money (taking care of number one) when she promised to help with her sister's birthday party (family cooperation).

Also, if a parent values cooperation and low hassle, he or she may shy away from enforcing a rule requiring cooperation because it will take a lot of effort. If you wish your children to cooperate, your job will be easier if your family rules support cooperation.

Effective rules reflect the ages and abilities of children. John McDermott, in his book *The Complete Book of Sibling Rivalry,* outlines four stages children go through in sibling relationships. He suggests responses and limits that are appropriate at different ages.

1. "Might equals right." Most preschoolers feel that the world centers around them. Since their world is controlled by big powerful adults, they often equate might with right. Parents begin to develop children's judgement by establishing and enforcing rules governing how to treat people. For example, "Touch gently. If you hit I will take you to your room." Parents can also introduce the next stage. "You can sometimes get what you want by making deals instead of fighting. Then you can both be happy."

2. "You scratch my back and I'll scratch yours." During early grade school, children shift in orientation from power and force to partial control through exchange of favors. Parents can encourage this cooperation by increasing the payoff. For example, "You kids are having trouble picking up the blocks. Find a way to cooperate, and we will go to the park when you are done."

3. "Law and order (or no fair cheating)." As children gain experience cooperating in specific situations, it becomes possible to make rules or agreements that can govern future events. The rules may be devised by children alone or with adult assistance. Children can abide by the rules, even when they are occasionally unfair, because they know they will be protected at other times. Using rules to decide what to do is the highest level of cooperation many adults attain.

4. *"Morally right."* Sometimes children in late adolescence develop a set of moral values they live by. In these cases a person is governed by what she or he thinks is right, rather than by "rules"or other people's opinions. Parents can encourage the development of an internal value system by talking about how other people feel, why they (the parents) make certain decisions, and respecting other people rather than taking advantage of them.

ESTABLISHING APPROPRIATE CONSEQUENCES

Setting age-appropriate limits as children grow older is challenging, particularly when you have children at different levels of development. One result, however, of developing rules is having them tested.

Most children test rules. It does not mean the children are bad or unruly, it simply means they want to know what will happen. When you establish a rule, give some thought to what the consequence will be when a child tests it.

Consequence differs from punishment. Punishment is something bad someone else does to you. Consequences result from your own behavior. For example, if a child touches a hot oven door and gets gets burned—that is a consequence of his action. If, on the other hand, he touches the door and gets spanked by an adult, that is punishment.

Consequences are most effective when they are immediate, consistently carried out, and related to the offending behavior. Let's look at each of these criteria briefly.

Effective consequences are immediate. Children learn best when feedback is quick. That way there is little confusion about what the consequence relates to.

Effective consequences are consistently carried out. Establish consequences you can carry out; follow through with the consequence each time the rule is tested. When the consequence is intermittent, children may try to break the rule hoping that they will get away with it this time.

Effective consequences are related to the child's behavior. Consequences are easier for the child to accept when they are related to the offending behavior. The relationship between the rule and the consequence may need to be expressed explicitly. For example, the relationship between "touch gently"and "or I will take you to your room,"can be related by "Treat people gently or you play alone. I can not let you hurt other people." In this case the child is being separated, not for "punishment,"but for protection of the other child. The child learns that to be with other people he must behave in a certain way. This is also illustrated in the following situation.

Sandy (age 7) and Cindy (age 6) were sisters. Their mother had recently taught them to negotiate. The girls were excellent at helping puppets solve their problems, however they did not use the approach with each other.

After getting thoroughly tired of the bickering, Mom told the girls that they must attempt to resolve their difficulties themselves. Further, if they were fighting over something near her, she would take it away and they could have it back only when they both agreed to a solution. Her rationale was, "I need more quiet. If there are things you are going to fight over, I will remove them so the reason to fight won't be there."

In Sandy and Cindy's home the rule was, "Cooperation is the key to success." In this case, to achieve the success of having the item, quiet for the parent and negotiation were necessary. Consequences are most effective when they are related to the rule and are carried out immediately and consistently. Exercise 6-3 is provided so you can practice identifying common errors in establishing consequences.

EXERCISE 6-3: Developing Effective Consequences (page 68)

Some children require more motivation than others, even with appropriate, consistent rules; we will look at some additional ways to encourage those children to negotiate.

EXERCISE 6-3: Developing Effective Consequences

Instructions: Read each situation and write a consequence. Remember that an effective consequence:
   (1) is related to the event,
   (2) offers a choice,
   (3) is acceptable to the adult, and
   (4) is provided immediately.

1. The whole family is about to go to the park. Danny and David begin to quarrel over which radio station they get to listen to. Dad says, "I am not up to listening to bickering.
    You may _____
    OR _____."

2. Kathy and Steve were fighting over the comics which they both wanted to read. Dad was trying to balance the checkbook. He said "Your noise is bothering me.
    You may _____
    OR _____."

3. Sara and Emily were fighting over whose turn it was to set the table. Mother was tired of waiting for them to set the table. She said, "In this family, we all cooperate.
    You may _____
    OR _____."

Possible answers:
1. You may decide which station to listen to pleasantly,
   OR I will turn the radio off.
2. You may resolve your difference quietly,
   OR quarrel elsewhere.
3. You may decide whose turn it is, set the table and eat with Daddy and me,
   OR I will set the table and you can go without supper.

Kids Can Cooperate

MOTIVATING UNWILLING CHILDREN

In the most perfect of worlds, all children would automatically recognize the value of cooperation and use problem solving techniques as soon as they are introduced. In the real world, there are some children who decline to use the techniques, even though they understand them.

Generally, in my experience, these are children who either have difficulty thinking of appropriate alternatives or do not see that there is a benefit from using the problem solving process. Many of the children take the position that the difficulty they have is due to "bad" or uncooperative people and not their responsibility at all.

Show how negotiation benefits them. A child may understand how the problem solving process works but not believe it will benefit them. A good way to show how it would be effective is to take situation after situation and show how the process would have helped. This approach is illustrated in the following example.

My son John is a bright child, but once he gets an idea, all else goes from his mind. I introduced him to the problem solving process when he was nine. He understood the concepts, but he did not put them into actions with his younger sisters, Emily (age 4) and Sarah (age 5).

When I asked him why he didn't use the ideas, he said they take too much time and don't work anyway. I began to watch my children's interactions more closely.

One day Emily was gone and Sarah wanted to play with her brother. She proposed several activities, all of which were turned down. Finally, after numerous interruptions, John went to his room and closed the door. Sarah, predictably, began to pound on his door a little later. Unable to concentrate, John erupted from his room and Sarah ran away—initiating a grand game of chase.

When I caught up with John and calmed him down, I was able to tactfully point out that he had spent the last hour trying not to play with Sarah. If he had spent five minutes making a deal with her and fifteen minutes playing with her, he would have been forty minutes ahead. Fortunately for us all, he began to be more aware of how his sisters' needs affected him.

Sometimes children who begin to see how problem solving benefits them may not be able to think of ideas when they need them.

Require the child to think of alternatives as a consequence of unacceptable behavior. Children, like adults, often have difficulty thinking of alternatives during a conflict time. One way to assist is to require children to think of different ways they could have handled the problem. Initially, it may be difficult for your children to think of any ideas. As they gain experience, you can increase the number of ideas required. If your children are having difficulty, encourage them to think of crazy ideas—often opening the mind to crazy ideas opens the mind to new, good ideas. For example:

My son (age 10) understood the process of problem solving in theory, but he had great difficulty finding alternatives for his conflicts. We established the family rule that when you hit your brother or sister, you have to go to your room and think of several alternatives to hitting. The alternatives did not have to be practical.

At first, he had to think of two alternatives. When he could think of two, we upped it to three and then five. Now, two years later, he is excellent at thinking of ideas. And can do so in a conflict situation as well as when he is calm.

Ask the child to see things from the other child's point of view. Some children have difficulty negotiating because they have no idea how the other child feels. You can help children become aware of feelings by labeling yours and discussing how other people's behavior affects your feelings. Or you can point out how other people's feelings are affected by your behavior.

You can also review for your child three ways to get information about how others feel: (1) observe face and body language, (2) listen to what a person says and how they say it, and (3) ask a person.

My daughter, Amy (age 10), was one of these children that just did not seem to understand how other people felt. One day she and her younger brother, Justin (age 7), were fighting over the TV. After listening to them bicker about what show to watch, I went in, turned off the television and sent them to their rooms. I told them that they could come out when they thought of a way to solve the problem that the other child would like. If they got stuck, they could ask for help. (The ideas did not have to be practical or acceptable to the originating child. I was asking them to think of something the other would like.)

The task was surprisingly hard for Amy. She truly could not think of any ideas she thought Justin would like. When she called for help, I asked her some questions that helped her think of what Justin would like. Interestingly, Justin had no trouble thinking of an idea.

After six or seven months of thinking of alternatives and looking at things from Justin's perspective, Amy was able to do some negotiating on her own. It is amazing how much difference that makes to their getting along.

In this example, Mom required both children to think of ideas the other would like. In this way she was encouraging them to become aware of the desires of their siblings.

Beginning a new skill like negotiation is difficult for most children. Learning is generally easier when children have a clear understanding of the process and receive support and encouragement from their parents. Children, both easy and difficult to motivate, benefit from having clear rules and consequences, and from hearing esteem-building messages. In the next chapter, we will wrap this topic up by looking at "who is responsible for happiness"; how adults can unknowingly encourage quarrelling and where to go if this approach doesn't work.

CHAPTER 7: WHERE DO WE GO FROM HERE?

I would like to tell you that once you teach your children to negotiate, peace will settle in your house. But that would not be true. It is possible that your children will always choose to negotiate their differences, but my guess is they will not always choose to cooperate.

Children who have the skills do not always choose to use them for several reasons. First, it takes time to incorporate the new skills into their lives; and second, children sometimes choose to be unhappy. I would like to look at these two issues and then consider how we may unknowingly contribute to sibling rivalry and what to do if you are still concerned about their quarrelling.

LEARNING TAKES TIME

Parents often assume that because children have successfully negotiated one or two conflicts, they can and will use their skills regularly. Realistically, it may take several months and sometimes a year or more for some children to incorporate the skills into their lives.

It takes time to internalize a skill. There is a large difference between understanding and experimenting with a skill, and adopting it as a part of one's self. It is sort of like learning a new language. You can study and pass the exams and talk to a foreign student, but it takes a lot of use before you begin to "think" in that language.

In Chapter 6 we looked at ways parents and teachers can encourage children to use the problem solving techniques. Of most importance is increasing children's self-esteem and developing rules that support cooperation as a way of life. While you are encouraging self-esteem and establishing consistent rules, keep in mind that children develop in their own patterns.

Children learn at different rates. Some children incorporate the negotiation skills in their repertoire very rapidly. Others adopt the material slowly. Each child has his own pattern. In the following example, one woman recalls her son's slow progress.

My son Kevin is a very creative child in many ways, but he is (or I should say was) socially blind. He could write fascinating stories, figure out complex math problems and design intriguing houses and ships, but he was stuck in dealing with other kids. This was particularly evident in dealings with his classmates on school projects and with his sister.

One of the main problems he had was latching onto the first good idea he had without considering other ideas from himself or others. He was convinced his ideas were best and would not listen to others. When someone tried to tell him what they wanted or a limitation of his idea, he would talk louder and faster, trying to convince them to accept his way.

Two years ago the only way he could think of to solve a problem with his sister was by hitting. When I asked him what else he could do, he had no idea. About a year and a half ago I began a campaign to help him look at a variety of options.

Whenever he got into trouble with his sister, he had to think of two things to do other than hitting. When we started, he could think of nothing, then he began to think of other ways to hurt his sister. I first permitted him to think of ways to hurt. When he could think of three of them, I asked him to think of different ideas. When he could think of three ideas that were not hurting, I upped the request to five and later to seven.

Now he can think of many ideas, and usually considers several ideas before he acts. This spring the process is really coming together for him. He is able to predict what will meet both his and his sister's needs and what probably will not. He generally listens when someone suggests an idea and tries to incorporate part of it in his idea.

Part of the change may be due simply to maturation, but I think a large part is the realization that it is often possible for both him and his sister to each get what they want.

WHO IS RESPONSIBLE FOR HAPPINESS?

Sometimes children, even when they are good problem solvers, will choose not to negotiate. This generally leads to one or more of the children being unhappy. When this happens, many parents feel torn between wanting to move in and make everyone happy, and letting children experience the results of their decisions. Before adults act, they may want to consider whether they are responsible for their children's happiness.

Mark is having a fit because he can't make a dump truck work. Susie and Anna are crying because Molly was mean and went home; worse yet, taking her new walkie-talkies they hadn't had a chance to play with. What's a parent to do? Try to console your children or shut yourself up in a soundproof room? I don't know the answer, but there is one thing I'm sure of: you can't *make* another person happy.

Happiness is a person's own choice. Many are the times I have tried to console my children, only to find they prefer to be unhappy.

I remember the time my husband and I took our son on a trip he wanted. He had both parents' attention for a full six hours. When I asked how he liked the day, he said, "It was terrible." He focused on the one incident all day that had not worked out as he wished. At that point I realized I could arrange events, but I could not make him happy.

You can control events, but you can not control a person's reaction to those events. If you change events to prevent or reduce your child's unhappiness, you encourage him to let others be responsible for his happiness. And if you make life too pleasant, you do not permit your child to develop skills for coping with frustration and disappointment himself.

Respect your child's feelings. Many people are uncomfortable when children show their emotions, but emotions are real. Children don't stop being afraid simply because someone says, "Don't be scared," or suddenly become happy because someone says, "Cheer up."

Clarify options for children. Children can become overwhelmed by their feelings, so you can try to help by clarifying their choices. For example, "You are disappointed Erin can't come over today. You can decide if you want to be unhappy or if you want to find someone else to play with." When you offer a choice, be sure you are willing for the child to choose it, and then respect the child's decision.

Help your child find self-comforting activities. Babies often learn to comfort themselves; as toddlers they may suck their thumbs or cuddle a blanket for comfort. As children grow older those comforts are often denied them. But everybody needs some ways to comfort or nurture themselves. Some possible activities are: sitting in a rocking chair, cuddling a stuffed animal, swinging on a swing, singing a song, reading a book or drawing pictures. Parents can encourage children by modeling taking care of themselves and explaining to children how they are taking care of their own needs.

Sometimes children need to experience being unhappy. I do not know why it is but some really neat, together kids occasionally choose to be miserable. It is almost as though they must practice being unhappy so they can really choose to be happy. This desire to be unhappy is illustrated in the following incident.

My daughter Elizabeth (age 6) is a very charming and capable girl. She is very good at getting her needs met in acceptable ways. It was very startling when one Saturday afternoon she became hysterical because her brother would not play with her. Her usual approach, if Richard would not play, was to play with a friend up the street, ask me or her Dad to play with her, or ask if she could help us.

I spent quite a while trying to discover what the problem was and offering her suggestions. Nothing seemed to help. I finally concluded that she wanted to be miserable and she was doing her usual excellent job. As I left her room, I told her it was okay to be unhappy if she wanted, and when she was done being unhappy she could come to me for ideas if she needed them. About two hours later she emerged from her room, cheerful and full of energy as usual.

For various reasons children sometimes choose to be unhappy. When adults clarify their childrens' options and respect their choices, children can learn to be responsible for their own feelings.

WHAT IF MY CHILD STILL HAS A PROBLEM?

Some children consistently choose a path that adults think is unhealthy. If that happens, the parents may choose to seek expert advice. This expert can be knowledgeable in learning styles, parenting skills or family counseling.

Have a physical exam. Sometimes children's unacceptable behavior is linked to physical problems. They may have difficulties in hearing or seeing, allergies, medication imbalance or something else that makes concentration difficult. One unruly teen reached tenth grade before a remedial reading teacher had his vision tested. When he got glasses he settled down, learned to read, and became an excellent student.

Check for a learning disability. People have different ways of learning. If a child is having difficulty learning both academic and social skills, you may wish to have him or her tested. Many children with learning disabilities can be taught how to transfer the material they are given into a form they can more easily learn from.

Arrange for a personal assessment. Many guidance and counseling centers have an initial assessment. This assesment is like a doctor's check up. They will tell you if they think the behavior pattern is normal or not. If not, they will outline the approach they would take to assist the child, and how long they expect the process will take. Asking for a personal assessment does not obligate you to follow their recommendations.

Consider counseling. Some children have problems that are beyond the scope of simple education. Those children need counseling and help reorienting themselves. If you choose counseling or therapy, choose a counselor you feel comfortable with and confident in. Talk to several people before you make your decision. Remember that the counselor who was great for a friend may not be great for you. It is sort of like choosing a parent, choose one that you can trust.

WHERE DO YOU GO FROM HERE?

I believe that life is a process of growth. Wisdom and maturity are not something that we have magically at 12, 18 or 21, they develop from experience. Our job as parents and teachers is to establish a framework in which people can grow. The most helpful ingredients in that framework are feelings of being lovable and capable. Children feel lovable when people like being around them and they hear affirming messages. Children feel capable when they can get their needs met in acceptable ways. The problem solving process we have presented offers children skills to meet their needs. When children feel lovable and capable, they can look for options that meet their own needs as well as those of others.

picture 2

Kids Can Cooperate

APPENDIX A: ASSESSMENT GAMES

The following are four games to help assess a child's understanding of the skills needed for problem solving. You may wish to use these assessment games with preschool children and with older children who have trouble picking up the problem solving concepts. The first game focuses on verbal concepts, the second on feelings, the third on generating alternatives and the fourth on predicting consequences.

The format may seem repetitive, however it is designed to be encouraging and supportive for the preschool child. A form to record your child's responses and a brief description of how to interpret the results follows the games. Two series of games are included so that you can retest your children without their remembering the questions.

━━ FIRST ASSESSMENT SERIES ━━

GAME ONE: BASIC VOCABULARY

Note for parents/teachers: The text for these games assumes the child will give a correct response. If the child gives an incorrect or inappropriate answer, repeat the question once. If the answer is still incorrect or inappropriate, go on to the next question.

1. **Is/not/or concepts**

    Materials: Picture #1. (Page 75)

    Instructions for child: *Now we are going to play three games with this picture. I will ask you some questions about this picture. First we will play a game about "is", "not" and "or."*

    a. *Kathy* (point to girl with a dress) *IS a _____.*
        (Wait for child's response.)
        Right, Kathy is a girl. Kathy IS NOT a ____.
        Right again, Kathy is NOT a boy/woman/etc.
        OR a _____, OR a _____.

    b. *Mike* (point to boy in the picture) *IS a _____.*
        (Wait.)
        Yes, Mike is a boy. Mike is NOT a _____.
        (Wait.)
        You're right, Mike is NOT a girl/man/etc., OR a _____, OR a _____.

2. **All/a/some concepts**

    Materials: Picture #1. (Page 75)

    Instructions for child: *Now we are going to play a game with "all", "a" and "some." I will ask you some questions and you will point to the answer.*

    a. *First we will hunt for dogs. Listen carefully.*
        Point to A dog. (Wait.) *Right, that is A dog.*
        Point to ALL dogs in the picture. (Wait.)
        Right, you pointed to all the dogs in the picture. (If child does not point to all the dogs, point to each child in the picture and ask "Does this child have a dog?" Then ask child to point to all the dogs again.)
        Point to SOME dogs. (Wait.) *Right, you pointed to SOME dogs, not ALL dogs.*

    b. *Now we will hunt for children with hats.*
        Point to A child wearing a hat. (Wait.) *Right, that is A hat.*

    Point to ALL children in the picture wearing hats. (Wait.) *Right, you pointed to all the children wearing hats.* (If child is wrong, respond as described in 2-a.)

    Point to SOME children wearing hats. (Wait.) *Right, you pointed to SOME children with hats, but not ALL children with hats.*

3. **Same-different concepts**

    Materials: Picture #1 (Page 75)

    Instructions for child: *Now, we are going to play a different game with this picture. We are going to look for things that are the same and things that are different.*

    a. *This pet* (point to a dog) *is a dog.*
        Point to the SAME kind of pet. (Wait.) *Right, that is the same kind of pet. It is a dog.*
        Point to a DIFFERENT kind of pet. (Wait.) *Right again. That is a DIFFERENT kind of pet. It is a _____* (repeat name).

    b. *This child* (point to child in baseball uniform) *is wearing baseball pants.*
        Point to a child wearing the SAME kind of pants. (Wait.) *Right, he has on baseball pants too.*
        Now, point to a child wearing DIFFERENT pants. (Wait.) *Right, he is wearing different pants.*

GAME TWO: RECOGNIZING FEELINGS

Materials: Picture #2 (page 76)

1. **Labeling feelings** (Show child Picture 2.)

    Instructions for child: *Now we are going to play another game. This game is about feelings.*

    a. *Point to a HAPPY face.* (Wait.)
        Right, that is a happy face.

    b. *Point to a SAD face.* (Wait.)
        Yes, that is a sad face.

    c. *Point to a MAD face.* (Wait.)
        Right, that is a mad face.

    d. Now point to a SURPRISED face. (Wait.)
        Right again, you found a surprised face.

2. Identify feelings of real people.

Note: Adult will need to act out the feelings. Most people find it easier to make realistic "feeling faces" if they think of a situation when they felt the emotion they are trying to act out.

Instructions for child: *I will make a face, and then you guess what the feeling is.*

a. Make a MAD face. Then ask, *What kind of a feeling was that?* (Wait.)
   Right, that was a mad/angry face.

b. Make a HAPPY face. Then ask, *What kind of feeling was that?* (Wait.)
   Right, that was a happy face.

c. Make a SAD face. Then ask, *What kind of feeling was that?* (Wait.)
   Right, that was a sad face.

d. Make a SURPRISED face. Then ask, *What kind of feeling was that?* (Wait.)
   Right, that was a surprised face.

3. Predicting feelings

Note for parent/teacher:
If the child gives an answer that seems inappropriate, ask the child, *"Why would you feel that way?"* If the answer is reasonable, accept it as correct.

Instructions for child: *I am going to tell you a story, and then ask you how you would feel if it happened to you.*

a. *How would you feel if someone grabbed your favorite toy away from you while you were playing with it?* (Wait.)
   Right, you would feel mad.

b. *How would you feel if you met a lion on the street?* (Wait.)
   Right, you would feel scared/surprised.

c. *How would you feel if you got something you wanted for a long time?* (Wait.)
   Right, you would feel happy.

d. *How would feel if someone you wanted to play with couldn't come over to play?* (Wait.)
   Right, you would feel sad/lonely.

GAME THREE: ALTERNATIVES

Materials: Picture #3

Instructions for child: *Now we are going to play another game. First I will show you a picture of two children, Amy and Brian. Then I'll ask you some questions about the picture. There are no right or wrong answers — I want your ideas about what happened.*

This is Amy (point to child wearing shorts) *and this is Brian* (point to child with the apple).

1. *What is happening in this picture?* (Wait for response.)
   If the child's response includes the feelings of the children, skip to Question 3.

2. *How do you think the children feel?* (Wait.)
   Respond appropriately; e.g., *Yes, one child feels sad and one child feels happy.*

3. *Why do you think Amy* (point to child wearing shorts) *feels sad?*
   (Wait.)
   Respond, *You think she feels sad BECAUSE....* (fill in child's reason).

4. *What could Brian* (point to child with apple) *do to help Amy feel happy?* (Wait).
   Respond, *Yes, he could...* (repeat child's response). *What else could he do to help Amy feel happy?*
   What else could he do to make Amy feel happy? (Continue waiting, responding and asking until your child runs out of ideas.)
   Summarize the child's ideas, e.g., *You thought of three things Brian could do to make Amy happy. He could...* (insert child's answers).

5. *Let's pretend Amy wants the apple a lot. What are SOME different ways she could get an apple?*
   (Wait.)
   If the child has ideas, respond and summarize as in Question 4.
   If the child does not respond, ask, *What is one way Amy could get an apple?* (Wait, respond. DO NOT evaluate ideas — that comes later.)
   Continue asking for ideas until child runs out. Then summarize alternative generated. For example, *You thought of four ways Amy could get an apple. He could...* (fill in child's responses).

GAME FOUR: PREDICTING CONSEQUENCES

Materials: Picture #3 (Page 79)

Instructions for child: *Now I want you to imagine what will happen if Amy tries some different ideas.* (Begin with ideas your child generated in Game 3, Question 5.)
What might happen if Amy —

GRABBED the apple. (Wait.) *Yes, Brian might cry/grab it back/tell mommy.*

ASKED TO SHARE the apple. (Wait.) *Right, Brian might share/not give it to her.*

ASKED HER MOTHER for an apple. (Wait.) *She might not have one/might say it's too near dinner.*

ASKED TO TRADE the apple for sugarless gum. (Wait.) *Brian might do it/say NO!*

TRIED TO MAKE A DEAL — I'll play ball with you if you share your apple. (Wait.) *Brian might do it/say no.*

picture 4

Following are four games to help assess a child's understanding of the concepts and skills needed for problem solving. Again, you may wish to use these assessment games with preschool children and older children who have trouble picking up the problem solving concepts. The first game focuses on language skills and concepts; the second, on feeling words and concepts; the third on the ability to generate alternatives; and the fourth, on the ability to predict consequences.

GAME ONE: BASIC VOCABULARY

Note to parents and teachers: The text for these games assumes the child will give a correct response. If the child gives a wrong or inappropriate answer, use the following procedure unless other directions are given: Repeat the question once and then go on to the next question.

1. **Is/not/or concepts.**

   Materials: none

   Instructions for child: *We are going to play a ~~ne~~ game about "is," "not" and "or."*

   a. *Daddy IS a _____. (Wait.)*
      Right, Daddy is a man. He is NOT a _____.
      (Wait.)
      Right again, Daddy is not a woman/boy/etc. OR a _____

   b. *Mommy is a _____. (Wait.)*
      Right, Mommy IS a woman/lady. She is NOT a _____.
      (Wait.)
      Right, Mommy is NOT a man/girl/etc. OR a _____

2. **All/a/some concepts**

   Materials: Picture #4. (Page 80)

   Instructions for child: *Now we are going to play another game with this picture. I will ask you some questions about this picture and you will point to the answer.*

   a. *First we will look for children with hats.*
      Point to A hat. (Wait.)
         Right, you pointed to a hat.
      Point to ALL the hats. (Wait.)
         Right, you pointed to all the hats.
      Point to SOME of the hats. (Wait.)
         Right, you pointed to some of the hats, but not all the hats.

   b. *Now we will hunt for children wearing pants.*
      Point to A child wearing pants. (Wait.)
         Right, the child is wearing pants.
      Point to ALL children in the picture wearing pants. (Wait.)
         Right, you pointed to all the children wearing pants.
      Point to SOME children wearing pants. (Wait.)

Right, you pointed to SOME children wearing pants, but not ALL children wearing pants.

3. Same-different concepts

Materials: Picture #4 (Page 80)

Instructions for child: *Now, we are going to play a different game with this picture. We are going to look for things that are the same and things that are different.*

a. *This child* (point to child who is holding a soccer ball) *is wearing a shirt with short sleeves.*
   Point to a child with the SAME length of sleeves. (Wait.) Right, he/she is wearing short sleeves.
   Now point to a child with DIFFERENT length sleeves. (Wait.) Right, he/she is wearing a different length sleeve.

b. *This child* (point to a child with long pants) *is wearing long pants.*
   Point to a child wearing the SAME length pants. (Wait.) Right, that is the same length of pants. They are both wearing long pants.
   Point to a child wearing a DIFFERENT length of pants. (Wait.) Right, that is a different length of pants. Those are shorts.

GAME TWO: RECOGNIZING FEELINGS

Materials: Picture #5 (Page 83)

Instructions for child: *Now we are going to play another game. This game is about feelings.*

1. **Labeling feelings.** (Show child Picture #5.)

   a. *Point to a HAPPY face. (Wait.)*
      Right, that is a happy face.

   b. *Point to a SAD face. (Wait.)*
      Yes, that is a sad face.

   c. *Point to a MAD face. (Wait.)*
      Right, that is a mad face.

   d. *Now point to a SURPRISED face. (Wait.)*
      Right again, you found a surprised face.

2. **Identify feelings of real people.**

   Adult will need to act out the feelings. To make the feelings more real it is often helpful to think of a situation when you felt the feeling you are acting out.

   Explanation for child: *First I will make a face, and then you guess the feeling.*

   a. Make a MAD face. Then ask *What kind of a feeling was that? (Wait.)*
      Right, that was a mad/angry face.

b. Make a HAPPY face. Then ask *What kind of feeling was that?* (Wait.)
    Right, that was a happy face.

c. Make a SAD face. Then ask *What kind of feeling was that?* (Wait.)
    Right, that was a sad face.

d. Make a SURPRISED face. Then ask *What kind of feeling was that?* (Wait.)
    Right, that was a surprised face.

3. Predicting feelings

Note for parent/teachers:
If a child gives an answer that seems inappropriate, ask the child, *"Why would you feel that way?"* If the answer is reasonable, accept it as correct.

Instructions for child: *I am going to tell you a story, then ask you how you would feel if it happened to you.*

a. *How would you feel if someone broke your new balloon on purpose?* (Wait.)
    Right, you would feel mad.

b. *How would you feel if you could not find your parents in a store?* (Wait.)
    Right, you would feel scared.

c. *How would you feel if someone said, "I like you lots"?* (Wait.)
    Right, you would feel happy.

d. *How would feel if your parents were sick a long time?* (Wait.)
    Right, you would feel sad/lonely/worried.

GAME THREE: ALTERNATIVES

Materials: Picture #6 (Page 84)
Instructions for child: *Now we are going to play another game. I will show you a picture of two children, Mary and Carla. Then I'll ask you some questions about the picture. There are no right or wrong answers — I just want your ideas.*
This is Mary (point to girl on the ground) *and this is Carla* (point to child standing).

1. *What happened in this picture?* (Wait for response.)

    If the child's response includes the feelings of the children, skip to Question 3.

2. *How do you think Mary feels?* (Wait.)

    Respond appropriately; e.g., *Yes, Mary feels hurt/sad/angry.*

3. *Why do you think that Mary feels hurt/sad/ mad?* (Wait.)

    Respond appropriately, e.g., *"You think she feels sad BECAUSE ... (fill in child's reason)."*

4. *What could Carla* (point to child standing) *do to help Mary feel better?* (Wait.)

    Respond, Yes, she could ...(repeat child's response). What else could she do to help Mary feel better?" (Wait.)

    What else could she do to help Mary feel better? (Continue waiting, responding and asking until your child runs out of ideas.)

    Summarize the child's ideas, e.g., *You thought of three things Carla could do to help Mary feel better. For example, she could ... (fill in child's ideas).*

5. *Let's pretend Carla wants the tricycle Mary has. What are SOME different ways she could get a tricycle?* (Wait.)

    If child has ideas, respond and summarize as in Question 4.

    If the child does not respond, ask, *What is one way Carla could get a tricycle?* (Wait, respond. DO NOT evaluate ideas—that comes later.)

    Continue asking for ideas until child runs out. Then summarize alternatives generated.

GAME FOUR: PREDICTING CONSEQUENCES

Materials: Picture #6 (Page 84)

Instructions for child: *Now I want you to imagine what will happen if Carla tries some different ways to get a tricycle.* (Begin with ideas your child has generated.)

What MIGHT happen if Carla —

    GRABBED the tricycle. (Wait.) *Yes, Mary might cry/grab it back/tell mommy.*

    ASKED TO SHARE the tricycle. (Wait.)
    Right, Mary might share/not give it to her.

    ASKED HER MOTHER for a tricycle. (Wait.) *She might not have one/might say it's too expensive.*

    ASKED TO TRADE a turn on the tricycle for sugarless gum. (Wait.) *Mary might do it/say NO!*

    TRIED TO MAKE A DEAL—I'll play ball with you if you share the tricycle. (Wait.) *Mary might do it/say no.*

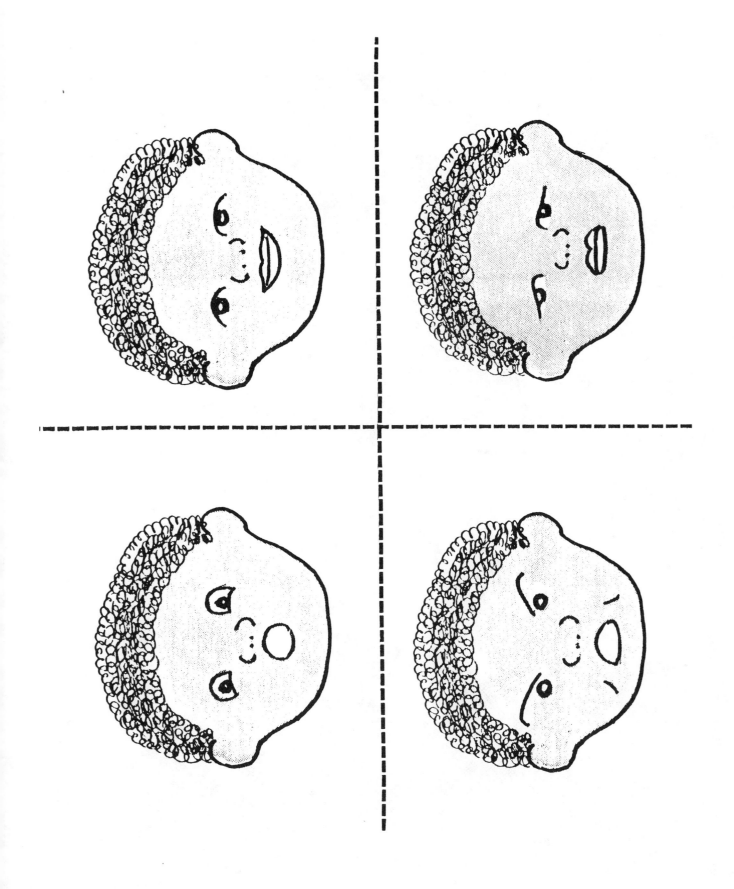

EVALUATING THE ASSESSMENT GAMES

You can use the sheet that follows to record your child's responses. Children have three levels of response to these questions. The first level is where they are not familiar with the terms or concepts. On the second level, the concepts are vaguely familiar—they intermittently answer correctly. On the third level, they consistently use the concepts and terms correctly. It is often difficult to distinguish between intermittent knowledge and complete knowledge. For the purposes of this evaluation, notice the questions your child missed and begin teaching those skills. Remember, the purpose of the assessment is to find out where to begin. If you start a little high, the child may be able to follow you, but it will be difficult rather than enjoyable.

Record Sheet for Assessment Games

Child's name: _____

GAME ONE: Basic Vocabulary

1. Is/not/or concepts: is ☐, not ☐, or ☐

   is ☐, not ☐, or ☐

2. All/a/some: a ☐, all ☐, some ☐

   a ☐, all ☐, some ☐

3. Same/different: same ☐, different ☐

   same ☐, different ☐

GAME TWO: Recognizing Feelings

1. Pictures: happy ☐, sad ☐, mad ☐, surprised ☐
2. Real faces: happy ☐, sad ☐, mad ☐, surprised ☐
3. Predicting: a. ☐, b. ☐, c. ☐, d. ☐

GAME THREE: Alternatives

1. What happened? _____
2. Feelings _____
3. Why? _____

4. What could child do to help?

   _____ _____

   _____ _____

   _____ _____

   _____ _____

5. Ways to get what child wants:

   _____ _____

   _____ _____

   _____ _____

   _____ _____

GAME FOUR: Predicting consequences

grabbing _____

asking to share _____

asking an adult _____

asking to trade _____

making a deal _____

_____ _____

_____ _____

PLACE TO BEGIN

_____

_____

_____

_____

_____

Record Sheet for Assessment Games

Child's name: _____

GAME ONE: Basic Vocabulary

1. Is/not/or concepts: is ☐,   not ☐,   or ☐
                         is ☐,   not ☐,   or ☐

2. All/a/some: a ☐,   all ☐,   some ☐
                         a ☐,   all ☐,   some ☐

3. Same/different: same ☐,   different ☐
                         same ☐,   different ☐

GAME TWO: Recognizing Feelings

1. Pictures: happy ☐, sad ☐, mad ☐, surprised ☐
2. Real faces: happy ☐, sad ☐, mad ☐, surprised ☐
3. Predicting: a. ☐,   b. ☐,   c. ☐,   d. ☐

GAME THREE: Alternatives

1. What happened? _____
2. Feelings _____
3. Why? _____

4. What could child do to help?

   _____   _____
   _____   _____
   _____   _____
   _____   _____

5. Ways to get what child wants:

   _____   _____
   _____   _____
   _____   _____
   _____

GAME FOUR: Predicting consequences

   grabbing   _____
   asking to share   _____
   asking an adult   _____
   asking to trade   _____
   making a deal   _____

   _____   _____
   _____   _____

PLACE TO BEGIN

   _____
   _____
   _____
   _____
   _____

APPENDIX B:
ACTIVITIES TO ENHANCE
PROBLEM SOLVING SKILLS

Problem solving ability, like any other skill, improves with practice. This appendix provides a number of activities to practice skills needed for problem solving. Many children find it easier to practice the skills when they are not emotionally involved in a conflict.

LIST OF GAMES

Listening Games:	1. Listening Time
	2. Guess What I See
	3. Sally Says
	4. Animal Game
Feeling Games:	5. Feeling Mirror
	6. How Would You Feel If...
Alternatives:	7. What Might They Do?
	8. Magic Beans
	9. Ball Fight
Consequences:	10. Why-Because Story
	11. The 'Why' Chain
	12. What Might Happen

GAME 1:
LISTENING TIME

Purpose: To practice careful listening.

Materials: None

Ages: 3 and up.

Introduction: We are going to play a listening game. Sit and make yourself comfortable. Listen to the sounds you hear outside. You may want to close your eyes.

After about a minute say "Sharing time. What did you hear?"

Variations:
1. Sit outside and listen to sounds in the neighborhood.
2. Sit in a park and listen to the "sound of nature."

GAME 2:
GUESS WHAT I SEE

Purpose: To practice careful listening.

Materials: None

Ages: 4 and up.

Introduction: I am going to describe something you can see in this room. When you think you know what I saw, raise your hand.

Examples: (Describing a television) It is larger than a child's head. It is rectangular shaped, partly metal and partly plastic, has knobs and dials, and it makes sounds and pictures.
(Curtain) It is very thin, partly blue, partly white, up high, above the poster, it moves when the wind blows in.
(Child's suitcase) It has green and blue on it. It has a zipper and a white handle and is round in shape.
(A throw pillow) Soft, sort of square shaped, blue on one side and tweedy on the other.

Variations:
1. Play in the car.
2. Play outside.

GAME 3:
SALLY SAYS

Purpose: To encourage careful listening.

Materials: None

Ages: 5 and up

Introduction: (This is a no-lose variation of "Simon Says.") We are going to play a game called "Sally Says." In this game you do whatever Sally says. If the leader says, "Sally says clap your hands," what do you do? (Wait.) Right, clap your hands. If I say, "Sally says turn around," what do you do? (Wait.) Right, turn around.

Okay, let's practice that. (Go through a series of actions saying "Sally says ...." Do the same actions you say. Actions you might use are listed below.)

Now I will make it more fun. Sometimes I will say "Sally says" and sometimes I won't. Only do the action when I say "Sally says." When I don't say "Sally says," be very still.

What do you do if I say, "Sally says clap your hands?" (You clap your hands and wait for their response.) What do you do if I say "Touch your toes?" (Pause and ask, "Did I say 'Sally says'? Wait for child to say no.) Then what do you do? (Wait.) Right, be still.

Let's practice again. Sally says pat your tummy. (Wait.) Now, stomp your feet. Good, you remembered to be still. OR, remember to listen carefully, then decide. (Repeat preceding paragraph.)

Call out a variety of actions, sometimes with "Sally says," sometimes without. Some actions you can use are:

touch your toes	wave your arms
jump up and down	make a face
hop on one foot	reach for the sky
clap your hands	stomp your feet
stick out your tongue	pat your tummy

GAME 4:
ANIMAL GAME

Purpose: To encourage careful listening.

Materials: None

Ages: 3 and up (with younger ages, call names slowly)

Introduction: We are going to play an animal game. Whenever I say "cat," you say "meow." If I say another animal, don't say anything. What do you do if I say "cat"? (Pause.) What do you do if I say "dog"? (Pause.)

Ideas: Continue listing animals. Occasionally say "cat." Some series you could use are:
Cat, dog, cow, cat, mouse, cat, pig, horse, dog, cat, duck, bear, lion, cat, dog, dog, elephant, tiger, cat, elephant, cat, kangaroo, dog, cat, hippopotamus, cat, cat, rabbit, koala bear, dog, cat, goat, sheep, cat.

Variations:
1. Dog: go through the same list barking for dog.
2. Cat & Dog: Child meows for cats and barks for dogs.
3. Single color: Call out color names. Tell child to say "apple" every time you say "red." (Or, banana for yellow.) Ideas: red, blue, yellow, red, green, blue, purple, orange, red, black, blue, red, red, brown, yellow, white, red, orange, green, blue, green.
4. Multiple colors: Call out colors. Tell child to say "apple" for red and "banana" for yellow.

GAME 5:
FEELING MIRROR

Purpose: To help recognize feelings.

Materials: Cardboard frame to represent mirror.

Ages: 3 and up (with younger ages, call names slowly)

Introduction: We are going to play a game about feelings. First, I will make a face that shows a feeling. And then you make the same kind of feeling face.

Okay, let's start. I will make a mad face. (Make a mad face.) Now you make the same kind of feeling face.

Repeat with different emotions: sad, happy, scared, proud, disappointed, excited. (Note: Remember to use both "positive" and "negative" emotions.)

Variation for small groups: Have first child make a face and second child "mirror" it. Then second child makes a face and third child mirrors it. Continue around the circle.

GAME 6:
HOW WOULD YOU FEEL IF ... ?

Purpose: To encourage children to predict feelings and recognize that people feel differently about the same thing.

Materials: None

Ages: 4 and up

Introduction: We are going to play a game about feelings. I am going to tell you a situation and you tell me how you would feel.

Let's begin. How would you feel if you woke up and your Mom said, "I'm glad you're my child. I love you."

If children have different responses, point out that people feel differently about the same thing and then ask some why they feel what they do.

Ideas: How would you feel if ...

you went out and the sky was green?
you woke up in the morning and there were ducks in your wading pool?
your mom just said, "We are going to the park today"?
someone grabbed the toy you were playing with?
you had ice cream for lunch?
your best friend moved away?
your dad just said, "You did a good job of cleaning your room"?

Variations:
1. Have children make faces rather than call out words.
2. Have children tell situations.

GAME 7:
WHAT MIGHT THEY DO?

Purpose: To introduce alternatives to children by helping them imagine what different people might do.

Materials: None.

Ages: 4 or 5 and up.

Introduction: I am going to tell you a problem. And then we are going to pretend we are different people, and guess what they might do in the same situations.

Situation:

1. Your younger brother has a new toy that you would really like to play with. You ask him nicely to use it and he says "No!" You still want to play with it.
   What might you do?
   What might your big brother/sister do?
   What might your granddad or grandmom do if they wanted to play with the toy?
   What might the smartest person you know do?
   What might the kindest person you know do?
   What might a magician do?
   What might Mr. Rogers do?
   What might a police officer do?
   What might Superman/Wonder Woman do?

Other situations:

2. You are sitting looking at/reading a book. Your little sister wants you to play with her. You really want to be left alone.

3. You are in the library waiting for your dad to get finished. Someone comes up and says, "Hi, Dummy. What'cha doing here?"

4. Your Mom just announced it is time to go shopping. You go immediately to the car so you can sit in the front seat. Your big brother sees you heading for the car, runs ahead of you and gets in the front seat.

5. Your sister just changed the TV channel away from the show you were watching?

GAME 8:
MAGIC BEANS

Purpose: To encourage children to think of alternatives.

Materials: None. (Or you can use puppets.)

Ages: 4 and up.

Introduction: I am going to read a story but I need your help. When I stop, you fill in the parts of the story I need.

Story:

Once upon a time in a magical land far away, there lived three children. Their names were: (1)_____, (2)_____ and (3)_____. 1 (Peter) was the oldest, he was almost 13 years old; 2 (Sara), age nine, was second and 3 (Mica), age six, was the youngest. They lived on a farm up in the mountains with their mother and father.

Once a month their parents went to town to get supplies. Usually Aunt Millie would come and stay with them. However, this time she was sick. The children asked if they could stay by themselves this time since they were very good at taking care of themselves.

Mom and Dad said they could stay alone as long as they promised two things. "First," Mom said, "promise to find solutions that work for all of you if you have any disagreements. And, second, stay away from the blue mice on rag hill."

Just before they left, Mom put a beautiful box on the kitchen table. She told the children, "If you have any problems, take a bean from the box, ask for what you need and drop it on the ground. The bean will grow into whatever you ask for."

The morning went well. All the children had fun. Shortly after lunch Sara noticed that Mica was gone. She asked Peter if he knew where she was. He did not. They hunted all over the house and farm, but they could not find her. Sara decided to ask a magic bean to get something that would help them find Mica.

Sara ran in and got three magic beans. When she got outside she picked one bean and put the rest in her pocket. She held the bean tightly in her hand, and said "I need a _____ (something that will help them find Mica. It could be a telescope, magic carpet, magic mirror, megaphone)," and threw the bean on the ground.

As soon as the bean hit the ground it gave off a puff of smoke. When the smoke cleared there was the _____(item named above, e.g., telescope) lying on the ground. Sara and Peter used it to find Mica. She was standing beside a tree up on the hill trying to reach something in the tree.

As soon at they found Mica, Peter ran over and asked, "Mica, what are you doing here? We were worried when we couldn't find you."

"Trying to get my Annie doll back," Mica replied.

"What is your rag doll doing in the tree?" Peter asked.

"I put her on the ground when I stopped to pick some berries. One of the blue mice took her up to his home in the tree. He won't give her to me. He says he found her and he's going to make a nest from her."

"Let me get this straight. One of the blue mice took your rag doll up in the tree to make a nest of it. Is that right?"

"Yes."

"What have you tried?" Peter asked.

"Telling him to give it to me, but he won't. And trying to get it, but I'm not tall enough. You try, Peter, you're bigger."

Peter stretched as tall as he could, but he wasn't quite tall enough.

"Maybe if Mica sits on your shoulders, she will be able to reach Annie," said Sara.

So Mica climbed on his shoulders, but they were still too short. "Darn," said Peter, "what are we going to do?"

The three children sat and thought for a couple of minutes.

"I have it!" shouted Sara.

"What?" Peter and Mica asked excitedly.

"The magic beans. I have two beans with me. We can ask for what we need to get it back. What should we ask for?"

The children thought of a couple of ideas. "We could get a telephone, talk to Mr. Mouse, and ask him to give it to us. We could reach the doll by _____ or _____ (climbing a ladder, using a rope, etc.), or we could trade by offering a soft _____ or _____ (pillow, sweater, towel).

"Now what should we ask for?" asked Sara.

"I want to grab Annie," said Mica.

"Okay, Magic Bean, we need _____ (first suggestion, e.g., a tall ladder)," Sara said, and then threw the bean on the ground. When the smoke cleared, there was a _____ on the ground. The children tried to reach the doll, but the blue mouse moved it farther away.

"I want my doll," sobbed Mica.

"We have one more bean," said Sara. "Shall we ask for something soft to trade?" Peter and Mica nodded. "Magic Bean, give us a _____ (something soft) please." When the smoke cleared, there it was, looking soft and snuggly.

Sara picked it up and showed it to the blue mouse. "Mr. Mouse, will you trade the doll for this?" The mouse shook his head and said he did not need the soft thing since he already had the doll.

The children felt mad. They had asked, grabbed and tried to trade, but nothing happened. The children sat down and thought of ideas.

"I know," said Mica. What do you think Mica's idea is? _____. (If the child's story is reasonable, finish it out. If not, continue below.)

"You watch and see." As they watched, Mica spoke to Mr. Mouse. He went and got the doll and gave it to her.

"What did you say to him?" Peter and Sara asked.

"I told him I wanted my doll and asked him what he wanted in exchange for my doll. Mr. Mouse thought a moment and said he wanted the _____ (first item, ladder) because it would make it easier to get things into his nest. I told him that if he got the doll quickly he could have both the _____ (ladder) and the _____ (pillow)."

-The End-

GAME 9:
BALL FIGHT

Purpose: To introduce alternatives to children.

Materials: Two puppets and a small ball (or other toy).

Ages: 3 and up (with younger children, limit the alternatives presented.)

Introduction: We are going to have a puppet show. The two puppets, Luke and Pati, both want to use the small ball. You will get a chance to help them solve their problem.

Skit

Narrator: Once upon a time there were two friends: Luke (he bows) and Pati (she bows). Usually they had lots of fun, but today they are having trouble. Both Luke and Pati want to play with the ball at the same time.

Luke: It's mine. (He grabs one side of the ball.)

Pati: No. It's mine. (She grabs the other side of the ball.)

Luke: Is not. (Luke pulls the ball, Pati pulls back.)

Pati: Is too! (She pulls harder.)

Narrator: What's the matter?

Luke: I want the ball. It's mine.

Pati: I had it first. Mine.

Narrator: Well, you have a problem. Luke, you want the ball; and Pati, you want the ball. What can you do so you can both have fun?

Luke: I don't know.

Pati: I don't know either.

Narrator: (Speak to the audience) Okay kids, let's help them out. What are some things they can do? (If the children have no ideas, recall a situation or story where several alternatives were used. When children are through offering ideas, turn to the puppets.) Pati and Luke, these children have several ideas for you. You could ...(list the ideas the children presented). What will you do?

Pati: I will ... (fill in one idea). Is that OK, Luke?

Luke: Yes.

Narrator: I am glad you found an idea that works for both of you.

Variations:

1. Repeat with small puzzle.
2. Repeat with small rag doll or stuffed animal.
3. Repeat with small truck.

GAME 10:
WHY-BECAUSE STORY

Purpose: To practice 'why-because' thinking.

Materials: none

Ages: 4 and up

Introduction: I am going to tell you a story about Martin. I want you to listen carefully and tell me why you think he did some things.

Story:

Martin enjoyed running and climbing and swimming, especially on hot summer days. But the thing he liked to do most of all in the summer was to go to the zoo. Today was a special day. His mom said that if it was not raining, they would go to the zoo. As soon as Martin woke up, he ran to the window and peeked out. What do you think he saw?

(WAIT for a response.) He saw water droplets on the window. How do you think he felt?

(WAIT for a response.) Right, he felt mad/sad (repeat what child said) BECAUSE he saw droplets on his window. As a matter of fact, he felt so mad/sad that he stomped around the room while he was getting dressed. He stomped to the dresser to get his clothes, he slammed his drawer closed, and he stomped to the closet. WHY did he stomp around?

(WAIT for a response.) Right, BECAUSE he felt mad. He made so much noise stomping that he woke up Robby, his little brother. Robby began to cry. WHY did Robby begin to cry?

(WAIT for a response.) BECAUSE he was scared/awakened by the noise. Martin was mad at the weather, but he was not mad at his brother. He tried to cheer Robby up. First he gave him a truck, then an old stuffed bear; but neither thing helped. Next Martin gave Robby a big hug. Robby stopped crying. WHY did Robby stop crying?

(WAIT for a response.) BECAUSE Martin gave Robby a big hug. Martin said, "Robby, I am sorry I scared you." Just then Mother came in. "Boys, I am glad you are up. We can go to the zoo as soon as you are dressed and have eaten breakfast."

"But Mom," Martin said as he pointed to the droplets on the window, "what about the rain?"

"Oh," Mom laughed, "that's not rain. I am watering the lawn."

Martin ran to the window and looked out. Sure enough, there were droplets on the window, but the sprinkler was on. How did Martin feel now?

(WAIT for a response.) Right, he felt glad/happy. WHY did he feel happy/glad?

(WAIT for a response.) BECAUSE he could go to the zoo after all.

GAME 11:
THE 'WHY' CHAIN

Purpose: To practice 'why-because' thinking.

Materials: Picture number 3. (Page 79)

Ages: 4 and up

Introduction: We are going to play a game called "The Why Chain." (Show your children the picture.) "This is a picture of Mandy and Brian. What do you think is happening? (WAIT for a response.)

"You think ... (Repeat what child said). WHY do you think ... (repeat child's opinion)?" (WAIT for a response.)

CONTINUE asking "why" as long as it is fun for your child. Stop at the first sign of frustration or tiredness.

AN EXAMPLE OF HOW THE CHAIN MIGHT GO:

You think Mandy wants Brian's apple. Why do you think Mandy wants Brian's apple? (WAIT for a response.)

You think Mandy wants Brian's apple BECAUSE she is hungry. Why do you think she is hungry? (WAIT for a response.)

You think Mandy might be hungry BECAUSE she didn't eat lunch. Why do you think she didn't eat lunch?

Varations:
1. Use pictures from problem solving books *(I Want It, I Can't Wait, I Want to Play,* or *My Name is not Dummy).*
2. Cut pictures from a magazine.

GAME 12:
WHAT MIGHT HAPPEN

Purpose: To practice predicting consequences.

Materials: Picture number 3. (Page 79)

Ages: 4 or 5 and up

Introduction: We are going to play a game of guessing consequences. Consequences are things that might happen. Sometimes there are lots of possible consequences. For example, suppose you were out running on the playground and fell down. What might happen if you fell down? (Wait for response and repeat it. For example, "Yes, you might hurt your knees.") What else might happen if you fell down? (WAIT for a response and repeat it. For example, "Right, you might tear your pants.")

CONTINUE repeating your child's ideas and asking the question as long as your child is having fun and can think of ideas.

Situation: This is Mandy (show picture). She wants Brian's apple.

What might happen if she ASKED BRIAN FOR IT? Wait for response. Yes, he might ... (insert child's prediction).

What might happen if she GRABBED THE APPLE? Wait for response. Yes, he might ... (insert child's prediction).

What might happen if she CRIED? Wait for response. Yes, he might ... (insert child's prediction).

What might happen if she OFFERED TO TRADE FOR SOMETHING? Wait for response. Yes, he might ... (insert child's prediction).

What might happen if she ASKED BRIAN TO SHARE THE APPLE? Wait for response. Yes, he might ... (insert child's prediction).

What might happen if she ASKED A GROWNUP FOR AN APPLE? Wait for response. Yes, the grownup might ... (insert child's prediction).

Variations:
1. Julie and Paul were playing outside. Julie was using the wagon and Paul wanted a turn. What might happen if ... (fill in phrases from above)?
2. Evan and Jason were playing in Evan's room. Jason was playing with Evan's building blocks. Suddenly Evan decided he wanted to play with them. What might happen if ... (fill in phrases from above)?

APPENDIX C:
ADDITIONAL SAMPLE DIALOGUES

The problem solving skills presented in this book can be adapted to a variety of situations and styles. This appendix includes examples of parents assisting children negotiate, parents assisting a child to look for alternatives with a child who is not present, and children solving problems without adult help.

In the examples where an adult helps children solve their conflicts, you might look at how the parent defines the problem and ways the parent keeps the child or children focused on the problem solving process.

Some of the examples in this appendix follow the process presented in this book closely and others do not. In both cases, look at the way people's needs are being met, for that is the essence of negotiation.

WINDOW POWER
Children only

Megan and Michael were riding in the back seat of the car. All of a sudden they began to quarrel.

Megan: Don't look out my window.
Michael: Why?
Megan: Because it is my window.
Michael: Well, I can look out if I want to.
Megan: No, you can't. It's mine.
Michael: Just because it's next to you doesn't mean it's yours. We can both look out each window. Isn't that a good idea?
Megan: NO!
Michael: Why not?
Megan: It is my window, and I want to say who can look out.
Michael: Oh. Well, may I look out your window?
Megan: Yes.

COLD IN THE CAR
Parent facilitates

Mom, Michael and Jeffrey were driving in the car. Michael, age 9, was warm and opened the front window. Jeffrey, age 6, sitting in the back seat, complained of being cold and ordered Michael to close the window. Tempers then flared.

Mom: Okay guys, we have a problem. Jeffrey is too cold, Michael is too hot and there is too much noise for me to drive safely. I am go-

ing to pull over and park the car until we can solve this problem.
(Mom pulls over and parks.)
Mom: Now, how can we arrange things so everyone is comfortable?
(no response)
Okay, I'll contribute an idea and then each of you will have a turn. My idea is to give Jeff my sweater so he can keep warm.
Jeff: It is my legs that are cold.
Mom: What is your idea, Michael? It can be reasonable or unreasonable.
Mike: Give Jeff Mom's sweater, and he can put it on and pull his legs up inside to keep them warm.
Mom: Okay. Jeff, your turn for an idea.
Jeff: Go home now and let me get long pants and a sweatshirt, then go to the store.
Mike: Now, I think Jeff should have thought...(Mom interrupts).
Mom: Right now we are thinking of ways to get out of this mess, not talking about how we could have avoided it. My idea, and it is crazy, is Mike and Jeff trade pants. Jeff wear Mike's long pants and Mike wear Jeff's shorts.
Mike: You can trade pants, it is your idea. Jeff, what is your next idea?
(No response)
I have another idea but I'm not saying anything until Jeff does.
Mom: Jeff, if you have no ideas you can pass. (No response) Okay, Mike, I guess Jeff is passing. I will tell my idea. You and Jeff can trade places so Jeff can have the front window closed, and you can have the back open. That way the cold air will not blow on Jeff.
Mike: We could go to the store very quickly and go home quickly.
Jeff: Yeah!
Mom: Will it really be okay to go quickly? Won't your legs get too cold?
Jeff: Well, I can sit in the front and Mike in the back.
Mom: Mike, is that okay?
Mike: Yes.
Mom: Yea! Congratulations to us for solving this problem.

PUPPET STAGE
Mother helps child look at her options.

Jane comes in and complains "Mom, Ricky took down my puppet stage."

Mom: What do you want me to do?

Jane: I want you to make him put it back up.

Mom: You want your puppet stage back up, and one alternative is to ask me to tell Ricky to put it up.

Jane: Right.

Mom: Before I do anything I want to know what other choices you have. What else could you do?

Jane: You could put it up.

Mom: You could ask me to put it up. What else could you do?

Jane: You could make Ricky do it.

Mom: You could ask me to have Ricky rebuild it. What else could you do?

Jane: Nothing.

Mom: You can't think of any other choices?

Jane: Right.

Mom: I think there are some other ideas that might work. Do you want to think of ideas or shall I ask Ricky?

Jane: I could do it.

Mom: You could put it together again.

Jane: We could both do it.

Mom: You could ask me to rebuild the puppet stage or ask Ricky to. You could build it yourself or we could all do it. What will you do?

Jane: I will ask Ricky to do it. If he won't, then you can make him.

Mom: You have decided to ask Ricky to rebuild the puppet stage. If he won't, you have other ideas to try.

Post script: Jane found Ricky had already put the puppet stage together.

SHE POKED ME
Parent facilitates discussion.

Rachel and Martin were sitting on the sofa together. Martin was reading and Rachel was sewing some doll clothes. There was a loud scream. Mother looks up and sees Martin about to hit Rachel.

Mother: Okay Martin, what is going on here?

Martin: She poked me with her needle.

Rachel: No, I didn't. He bumped into my needle.

Martin: How could I bump into it if I was reading? Huh?

Mother: I can see you were hurt. I would like you to look at what options you have. What could you do to let Rachel know you don't like to be hurt?

Martin: I could poke her, and show her what it feels like.

Mother: You could poke her, what else could you do?

Martin: I could punch her or hit her.

Mother: You have thought of three ways to hurt her, what is something different you could do?

Martin: I could ignore her, but I don't want to.

Mother: You could hurt her or you could ignore her, what else could you do?

Martin: I could tell you, but you wouldn't do anything.

Mother: You could tell me, what else could you do?

Martin: I don't know.

Mother: Okay. You could hurt Rachel, ignore her, or tell me, what will you do?

Martin: I'm not sure.

Mother: None of those ideas look good to you. Can you think of something else?

Martin: Yeah. Demand she apologizes.

Mother: What would happen if you demanded an apology?

Martin: She'd say, "No!"

Mother: What else could you do?

Martin: I suppose I could ask her.

Mother: What do you think would happen?

Martin: If I was pleasant, she probably would apologize.

Mother: Are you ready to make a decision?

Martin: Yeah. I will ask her to apologize and move over so it won't happen again.

WINDOW NEGOTIATION
Dad assisting two children

Mark, Kevin and family were just starting vacation. Mark had his window open and was drawing. Kevin was trying to listen to his tape recorder with an ear plug.

Kevin: Mark, please roll up your window.

Mark: No.

Kevin: Please. With the window open I can't hear the tapes.

Mark: No. I will be too hot.

Kevin: This is going to be a long trip. To make it pleasant we must cooperate.

Mark: My closing the window isn't *both* cooperating.

Kevin: You can close the window and Dad can put the vent on.

Mark: No.

Kevin: We can alternate. Thirty minutes open and thirty minutes closed.

Mark: No. One hour open and one hour closed.

Dad: I am glad you fellas are negotiating. Unfortunately I need the window closed because the sound is making it difficult for me to drive well.

Mark: That's okay. If we have the vent on, it will give air when the car is stopped. The window doesn't.

CANDY DAY PROBLEMS
Mom helped her daughter look for alternatives.

Emily is permitted to have candy one day a week, usually Saturday. The candy is limited to once a week except for special occasions. A school friend frequently offers her candy at lunch time. Emily told her mom that she did not know what she should do.

Mom: What are some things you could do?
Emily: I could take it and give it to another friend.
Mom: True, what else could you do?
Emily: Give the candy to a teacher or the principal.
Mom: You thought of several people you could give the candy to. What is something different you could do?
Emily: Change candy day to a school day or (hopefully) have candy every day.
Mom: You could give someone else the candy, change candy day to a school day, or ask to do away with candy day. What else could you do?
Emily: Put it in my lunch box and bring it home.
Mom: Uh huh.
Emily: Or I could throw it away.
Mom: What else could you do?
Emily: I could ask my friend to have her mom give her one candy day too.
Mom: What else could you do?
Emily: I don't know.
Mom: You thought of lots of ideas. You could give it to someone, take it home, throw it away, change candy day, eliminate candy day, or ask your friend's mother to give her a candy day. What will you do?
Emily: I don't know. What should I do?
Mom: You have to make that decision yourself. The only idea I have to add is to tell your friend that you can't have candy unless it is candy day. Thank her and give her back the candy. Next time she offers you candy you can decide what you want to do.

COLORING BOOK
Mom helps children negotiate.

Christmas had been bountiful. Among many gifts, Rebecca, age 4, received a coloring book complete with stickers and new crayons. Ruth, age 7, received an activity book consisting of mazes, word puzzles, etc. Late Christmas day, when Rebecca went to use her new coloring book, she found that Ruth had completed about half the pages. Rebecca was mad and went crying to Mom. Mom sat down with Rebecca and Ruth.

Mom: Ruth, this family has a rule about possessions. If you wish to use something that belongs to someone else, you *must* ask first. We don't just use it. I feel it is necessary for you to compensate Rebecca somehow for your use of her coloring book. One idea is that you can use your money to buy her another coloring book, and then you keep this one.
Ruth: I don't want to.
Mom: If you don't like that idea, you can think of three ways to make it up to her.
Ruth: I can't think of anything.
Mom: That is fine. You can use my idea.
Ruth: No. I don't like it.
Mom: Well then, you can think of three ideas.
Ruth: Okay, I could give her my new activity book.
Mom: You could give her your activity book. What else could you do?
Ruth: I don't know.
Mom: That is fine. You don't have to do it right now. You have until supper to think of three ideas, and you may use my idea as one of yours.
Ruth: Mom, I don't use my Bonnie Doll Color Form much any more. She really likes that. I could give it to her.
(Rebecca smiles at that idea.)
Mom: True, you could give it to her. That's two ideas.
Ruth: I could read her a story. (Rebecca frowns.)
Mom: You thought of three ideas. How do you think she would like the activity book?
Ruth: I don't know, it is really too hard for her.
Mom: How do you think she would like the color forms?
Ruth: She might like it. She uses it a lot. But then it wouldn't be mine.
Mom: True. How do you think she would like a story?
Ruth: She likes it when I read her stories. But one story is too short. I should read her two stories. She might like that.
Mom: Are you ready to ask Rebecca?
Ruth: Yes. (She turns to Rebecca who had listened quietly to the whole exchange.) Which do you want me to do?
Rebecca: The Bonnie Doll Color Form. And you can still use it.

Post script: The rest of the afternoon was spent with both girls working on the coloring book. Ruth punched out the stickers so Rebecca could put them in.

VACUUM NEGOTIATION
Children problem solving alone.

Amy was tired of doing her jobs, so she decided to trade with someone else.

Amy: John, could you do my jobs if I vacuum one room for you?

John: No, because just one room is not very much.

Amy: Okay, two rooms.

John: Yeah. How about the dining room and the living room?

Amy: That's okay. I used to vacuum the whole house.

John: No, you didn't. Daddy did.

Amy: Yes, I did. How would you like to change jobs with me?

John: It is okay by me.

Amy: Good, I like vacuuming better than my jobs. But it might be just for this week.

John: Okay. And if you still want to trade next week, I have a bridge I would like to sell you.

WHO WILL SHUFFLE
Children negotiate alone.

Steve and Andy were arguing over who should shuffle the cards to play "Go Fish."

Steve: I want to shuffle.

Andy: No, they're my cards.

Steve: Let me shuffle.

Andy: No.

Steve: If you let me shuffle, I will let you go first.

Andy: Okay.

SLEEPING ARRANGEMENT
Dad helped Kevin decide how to negotiate with his sister.

Grandma and Granddad were visiting for vacation. They were sleeping in Anna's room, and she was sleeping in a sleeping bag in her brother's room.

Kevin: Dad, Anna insists on sleeping in the lower bunk and I don't want her to.

Dad: What did you try?

Kevin: I asked her to sleep in the corner where she slept before. She said, "No." I told her it was my bed and I could say who sleeps in it. She said she could sleep there since Grandma was sleeping in her bed. I told her if she wouldn't move I would tell you.

Dad: Kevin, you thought of three ways to get what you wanted. That's good. What I want now is for you to find out why she wants to sleep in the lower bunk and then find something that works for both of you. I suggest that you approach her as though you expected her to cooperate rather than to be difficult.

Kevin: (Speaking to Anna before he starts to negotiate) Anna, Dad says we need to work this out ourselves. I know we can because you are good at solving problems.

Anna: I want to sleep on the lower bunk.

Kevin: Why do you want to sleep there?

Anna: Because the floor is too hard.

Kevin: Oh. You could use the air mattress.

Anna: It's not as comfortable as the bed.

Kevin: You can move the mattress off the bunk and put it on the floor.

Anna: It's too hard for me to do.

Kevin: I can help you.

Anna: Okay.

SOFA ARRANGEMENTS

Mike and Erin were arguing over who got how much of the sofa. Mike wanted to lie down on most of the sofa, Erin wanted to sit on the same part and play with her dolls. The children were trying to negotiate themselves but were having trouble. Mom decided to help them.

Mike: If that proposal is not acceptable to you, tell me a proposal that is acceptable to you.

Erin: You move your feet and sit up properly.

Mom: What did you suggest?

Erin: That he sit up properly.

Mom: Mike, you want to lie down and Erin wants you to sit up properly.

Mike: (To Erin) What skin is it off your nose for me not to be sitting properly?

Erin: (No answer)

Mike: What difference does it make to Erin how I sit?

Erin: (No answer)

Mom: May I make a suggeston? (children nod) I think that there is a different issue involved. And I think the issue is what Mike said earlier. He is bored and Erin, I think, is also bored. Erin, is part of the problem that you want to play with Mike?

Erin: No, I want to sit like this.

Mike: You want to sit in the middle?

Erin: Uh-huh.

Mike: If you sit in the middle, I can't have my legs stretched out. I want to stretch my legs out.

Mom: Okay kids, Mike wants to stretch out on the sofa and Erin wants to sit in the middle. What can you two do?

Erin: I can sit on his legs.

Mom: Yes, you can. What's another idea?

Erin: He can put them on top of my lap.

Mom: He can put them on top of your lap. Mike, are you willing to try her second proposal?

Mike: What was her first proposal?

Mom: First, that she sits on your legs; and second, that you put your legs over her lap.

Erin: No, I don't think I like the second one.

Mike: Well, I don't want you to be sitting on top of my legs. It's okay if I put my legs on her lap but not the other way around.

Erin: It has to be the other way around.

Mom: Okay, Erin, do you remember what I said? You have to cooperate. Mike has given you several ideas and you have given him only one. He suggested that he move his legs up and you sit here—

Mike: No, that wasn't my idea. I move my legs up and she sits down *there* (points to the end of the sofa).

Erin: But then I couldn't play!

Mike: Why couldn't you play down there?

Erin: How can you reach down there from sitting?

Mom: Here is another idea—

Mike: Wait, I don't understand what you are saying. You would sit right *there* (again points to end of sofa).

Erin: And how can you play on the floor keeping your bottom down on the sofa?

Mike: I don't understand...

Mom: She wants to play on the same level. If she sits on the sofa she can play there where the stuff is.

Mike: She can play on top of my legs.

Erin: Un-un.

Mike: Erin, I have offered many possiblities. You have only offered one. You have to offer many minus one to be even.

Mom: Let's use numbers. How many is many?

Mike: Three, four, five?

Mom: Your five ideas are?

Mike: Okay. She could sit on the end and play on my legs. Or she could sit in another chair and play there.

Mom: That wasn't one of your ideas, but that is okay.

Mike: She goes someplace else.

Erin: No-o-o-o-o! That's not a good idea. Have him go to his room.

Mom: It's okay honey. He is listing ideas, not deciding.

Mike: Uhhhh, well that's three ideas. Ummmm...

Mom: She has suggested you go to your room, that you sit up, and that she sits on your legs. So far you are even.

Mike: Uh-o-o-o-oh.

Mom: Just for the record.

Mike: So I guess it is my turn to offer an idea. Well, I agreed to one of her ideas, so I don't think she should change.

Mom: Her idea was not a final decision. I was just asking for ideas. May I offer a couple of suggestions?

Mike & Erin: Yes.

Mom: One, we put two cushions on the floor and Mike will lie down cosily on the floor and Erin can play on the sofa.

Erin: Yes.

Mike: No-o-o-o. That's not a fair idea.

Mom: Mike, we are strictly looking at ideas.

Mike: Well, that seemed like a tilted idea to me.

Mom: The next idea is that we clear off the magazine table and put it in front of Erin so she can sit there (points to end of sofa)...

(Simultaneously) Mike: Yeah. Erin: No-o-o.

Mom: ...and play in front of her. Now, she thinks that's tilted for you. Another idea is that both children go to their rooms until they can come up with five ideas—

Mike & Erin: Nope!

Mom: That idea is tilted towards...?

Mike: Mom.

Mom: True. Another would be to bring the table in from the rec room so we can use that. Another idea is that we tilt up the end of the cushion so we can make Erin a little nest and protect Mike. Another idea is that we abandon the sofa altogether.

Mike & Erin: No-o-o-o.

Mom: Alternatives are only ideas. They have not been chosen yet. Oh, another idea— time share.

Mike: No.

Erin: Yes.

Mike: Maybe. (He moves into the disputed space; Erin screams.)

Mom: (Looks at the kids.) You have a choice. You can sit and negotiate, or you can each go to your own room until you can think of five different ideas.

Mike: I was only trying to get comfortable.

Mom: Okay Mike, let me put your situations this way. You may NOT sit in that seat unless you (1) negotiate, or (2) go to your room and come up with five new ideas.

Mike: Okay, I have an idea for something we can do. I can't really explain it—can I show you? (She nods.) Erin, we go back to sitting the way we were. And you do this. (She turns and sits parallel to Mike, between him and the back of the sofa. Erin puts her stuff on the back of the sofa.) Now are you comfortable? (Erin nods.)

Erin: Un, huh. (giggle) I am the meat in a sandwich.

Mike: I think we are having fun.

Mom: Are you guys doing well enough so we can call it an end?

Erin: Yes-s-s.

Mike: Now we have to get back to what we were doing before you got called in. Reading and playing.

Mom: Fine, and if you need more space you can move the back cushion off the sofa.

Kids Can Cooperate

APPENDIX D: BIBLIOGRAPHY

Siblings and Problem Solving Books

Acus, Leah Kunkle. *Quarreling Kids,* Stop the Fighting and Develop Loving Relationships Within the Family. Prentice-Hall, 1981.

Ames, Louise Bates. *He Hit Me First*. Dembner Books, 1982.

Calladine, Carole and Andrew. *Raising Brothers and Sisters Without Raising the Roof*. Winston Press, 1979.

Crary, Elizabeth. *I Want It, I Can't Wait, I Want to Play,* and *My Name is Not Dummy*. Parenting Press, 1982 and 1983.

Hendricks, Gay and Russel Wills. *The Centering Book*. Prentice-Hall, Inc., 1975.

McDermott, John F. *The Complete Book of Sibling Rivalry*. Wyden Books, 1982.

Shure, Myrna and George Spivac. *Problem Solving Techniques in Childrearing*. Jossey-Bass Publishers, 1978.

Child Guidance Books

Crary, Elizabeth. *Without Spanking or Spoiling:* A Practical Approach to Toddler and Preschool Guidance. Parenting Press, 1979.

Dinkmeyer, Don and Gary McKay. *The Parent Handbook,* A Systematic Training for Effective Parenting (STEP). Random, 1982.

Faber, Adele and Elaine Mazlish. *How to Talk so Kids Will Listen & How to Listen so Kids Will Talk*. Avon Books, 1982.

Lerman, Saf. *Parent Awareness Training,* Positive Parenting for the 1980's. A & W Publishing, Inc., 1980.

Self-Esteem Books

Dorothy Briggs. *Your Child's Self-Esteem*. Double Day, 1975.

Clarke, Jean Illsley. *Self-Esteem: A Family Affair*. Winston Press, 1978.

SUMMARY OF THE SIGEP APPROACH

The term SIGEP summarizes the steps involved in problem solving. Each letter stands for a particular step: Stop, Identify, Generate, Evaluate, and Plan.

1. STOP AND CALM YOURSELF

As soon as you know you have a problem, stop and look for options. If you are so upset that you have difficulty thinking, use one of the following methods to calm down. You can be angry and still think.

Count to ten   *Pretend you have a protective shield*
Take three deep breaths   *Run around the block*
Let the anger drain out   *Tell yourself "I am a capable person, I can work this out."*
Visualize yourself calm

2. IDENTIFY YOUR PROBLEM

It is easier to solve a problem if you have a clear understanding of it. This is done by gathering data and deciding what your own and other people's needs are.

Gather data— ask yourself:

What was happening before the conflict? What do I feel like? What do I want? What do other people involved in the situation want? Who else is this a problem for?

Define the problem.

1. Focus on the *specific behavior* that is difficult for you. (For example, "he is mean" might become, "he grabbed the books away from me.")
2. Distinguish between "wants" and "needs." ("I want that cake," "I need something to eat.")

3. GENERATE LOTS OF IDEAS

Write down all your ideas. Evaluate them later; evaluation stops the creative process. The ideas you write down first will probably be the ones you already had. When you run out of ideas, think of some silly or impractical ideas; that will help get new ones flowing.

Questions to stimulate ideas are:

What can I do differently? How can I change the physical setup to remove the problem? Who can help me? How can I prevent this from happening again? Can I buy or trade for some assistance?

What might other people do? What would the smartest person I know do? What would the kindest person I know do?

What are some crazy ideas? What might someone from outer space do? What could I do if I was a magician? What is the silliest idea I can think of?

4. EVALUATE YOUR IDEAS

Now is the time to evaluate the alternatives.

Look at the consequences. What will happen with each of the ideas? Will it achieve what you want? How will it affect other people? What problems will it have?

Consider how you would implement the idea. How much will it cost? How long will it take? How much energy will it take? Who else will be involved?

Is this a win-win alternative? Will this idea work for all the people involved?

Choose a plan. Choose the idea that best meets your need. Keep the list of ideas so that, if your choice doesn't work, you have a head start on choosing another.

If no idea is acceptable, consider how the ideas could be changed to make them acceptable.

5. PLAN HOW YOU WILL IMPLEMENT YOUR IDEA

Plan how you will implement the idea and when you will evaluate your plan.

Plan implementation. What things will you need for your idea? Do you need someone's permission or assistance? What will you do first?

Set aside a time to evaluate your plan. Decide on a time to review your plan and see if it is successful. If the solution is not working, choose another idea or return to identify the problem. If it is successful—

Pat yourself on the back.

SUMMARY OF PARENT'S OPTIONS
WHEN KIDS QUARREL

When children quarrel, parents have five options. They can ignore the quarreling, restructure the environment, direct the children's behavior, offer choices, or help children negotiate.

IGNORE UNDESIRABLE BEHAVIOR

How to ignore: Ignoring is most effective when you both ignore the offending behavior and give attention to desirable behaviors. A person ignores a behavior by acting as though the undesirable behavior does not exist. Often people find it easier to ignore annoying behavior if they concentrate on some pleasant thoughts.

When to ignore: Ignoring is appropriate when children are fighting for attention and when the fighting is not physically or emotionally harmful to either child.

RESTRUCTURE THE ENVIRONMENT

How to restructure the environment: Look for ways the quarreling can be reduced by removing things, adding things, or changing the way things are arranged. For example, if an older preschooler is upset because a toddler always gets into his books, the books could be stored up high or in the older child's room.

When to restructure: Restructuring the environment is appropriate when the conflict can be eliminated or reduced by changing the environment.

DIRECT CHILDREN'S BEHAVIOR

How to direct: Decide *specifically* what you want the child to do in place of what they are doing. For example, "Don't hit your sister" is unclear, while "Touch gently" is specific. Further, tell the child what you want in a way that makes it clear you like her, while making it equally clear that she needs to change her behavior. For example, "Sarah, when you want to hit Ruth come and tell me. I will help you figure out what to do."

When directing is appropriate: Directing behavior is appropriate when the situation is unsafe, children have few social skills, or the parent is too tired to offer choices or help children negotiate. It is also appropriate when children need "how-to" information or are too tired to make reasonable decisions.

OFFER CHOICES

How to offer choices: Decide what the child can do instead of what he is doing. The choice may be between two desirable options, or between the desired behavior and the consequence of not doing it. For example: "You can play pleasantly or play in your room." Offer only choices you are willing for the child to accept. If you are not going to throw away the toys, do not offer the choice "Pick up your toys, or I will throw them away."

When to offer choices: Offering choices is appropriate when the situation is safe and the parent has the time to offer choices. Simple choices like, "Give Mark the truck or I will give it to him" can be offered to non-verbal children.

ENCOURAGE PROBLEM SOLVING

How to encourage problem solving. Adults can help children negotiate by asking them to identify their problem, generate alternatives, to predict consequences of the alternatives and to make a decision. This process is described more fully in the summary sheet "How to Facilitate Children's Problem Solving."

When to encourage problem solving: Encouraging problem solving is appropriate when children have had experience with making decisions and have the background skills needed (listening, idea generation, and idea evaluation).

Summary Sheets

SUMMARY OF
HOW TO FACILITATE CHILDREN'S PROBLEM SOLVING

The primary job of an adult facilitator is to help the children remain focused on the problem and the problem solving process.

1. GATHER DATA

Collect information about events and feelings. Decide what parental options you will use. If you plan to help the children negotiate, avoid blaming anyone (even if you think someone is at fault). You may find the following questions useful:

What happened?   *How did you feel when you ... ?*
Why did you ... ?   *How did you feel when your friend/sibling ... ?*
What happened then?

2. STATE THE PROBLEM CLEARLY

It is easier for children to solve a problem if you have a clear understanding of the problem. State the problem in terms of both children's needs. You might wish to use either of the following approaches or develop your own.

Some questions: You want to _____ and your friend wants to _____. What can you do so you can both be happy?
   OR
I know you are both upset about what happened. I do not want to focus on that. I want to focus on what we can do *now*. What are some things we might do so that both of your needs will be met?

Remember: Include both (all) children's needs in the problem statement.

3. GENERATE LOTS OF IDEAS

Go for quantity of different ideas, not quality in this step. Write the ideas down if you can't remember them. Encourage children to suggest silly ideas as well as practical ones.

Write down all the ideas. Evaluate them later, evaluation stops the creative process.

Encourage different ideas. If a child offers similar ideas, tell the child how they are similar and ask her for something different. For example, "Hitting, punching, and biting are all hurting ideas, what is something different?"

Avoid criticizing ideas. If the child offers an idea you do not like, help him evaluate the idea in the next step.

Review the problem frequently. It is easy for kids to wander from the problem; remind them what the problem is. For example, "Yes, that is a problem too. Right now we are looking for ways to _____. When we are done we can consider that."

Focus on the childrens' ideas. Resist the temptation to add your ideas unless you are asked. If you offer lots of good ideas, children will depend on your skill rather than developing their own.

Focus on content, not grammar. Do not correct children's grammar directly. When you summarize you can restate the suggestion correctly.

4. EVALUATE THE IDEAS

Look at the consequences. Encourage children to consider the question, "What might happen if you _____ ?" OR "How will Mary feel if you _____ ?"

Is this a win-win alternative? Will this idea work for all the people involved?

If no idea is acceptable, consider how the ideas could be changed to make them acceptable.

5. ASK FOR A DECISION AND HELP CHILDREN PLAN

List the alternatives, ask the children for a decision, help them plan how to implement the idea, and decide on a time to evaluate your plan.

List the alternatives. Remember to include them all: the ones you like and don't like.

Plan implementation. What do the children need to do first? Will the children need someone's permission or cooperation?

Plan time to evaluate. Decide on a time to review your plan and see if it is successful. If the solution is not working, choose another idea or return to identify the problem. If it is successful—

Congratulate the children on finding a solution and remind them if it does not work out there are other ideas.

Kids Can Cooperate

WITHOUT SPANKING OR SPOILING
By Elizabeth Crary

A Practical Approach To Toddler And Preschool Guidance--Author and parent educator Elizabeth Crary has taken the best ideas from four major child guidance approaches and combined them in one practical resource guide which is:

■ **Full of Ideas**--ways to reduce parent-child conflicts.
■ **Easy to Understand**--simple language and realistic examples make the information come alive.
■ **Appropriate for Young Children**--material was adapted specifically for use with toddlers and preschoolers.

PICK UP YOUR SOCKS...and other skills growing children need
By Elizabeth Crary

Tools and insights help you distinguish between obedience and responsibility and when each is appropriate. Look at skills kids need for household jobs, school work, and independent living (like resisting peer pressure and managing anger).

■ **Act effectively**--Makes discipline easier, gives guidelines for effective consequences for unacceptable behavior.
■ **Understand your kids**--A job chart lists average ages children do specific household tasks
■ **Feel confident**--Easy-to-use real-life examples and exercises give you the words you need to put ideas to work.

Order Now

PARENTING PRESS INC., P.O. Box 15163, Dept. 400, Seattle, WA 98115

Please send me:

____ Kids Can Cooperate $9.95
____ Without Spanking Or Spoiling $9.95
____ I Want It $4.95
____ I Can't Wait $4.95
____ I Want to Play $4.95

____ My Name Is Not Dummy $4.95
____ I'm Lost $4.95
____ Mommy, Don't Go $4.95
____ Children's Problem Solving Series $29.70
____ Pick Up Your Socks $11.95

(Prices subject to change.)

Enclosed is my check for _____ (payment must accompany order)

Name _____

Address _____

City _____ State ____ Zip _____

Order Subtotal	Add Shipping
$0--$10	$2.00
$10-$25	$3.00
$25-$50	$4.00

WA residents add 8.1% sales tax

Help Children
Solve Social Conflicts

Jason has a toy. Amy wants it. David can't find anyone to play with him. Kelly is tired of waiting for her turn on the swing. Sound familiar? Of course it does. All of us have found ourselves in the role of negotiator in our children's conflicts. Children's Problem Solving books can make that job easier.

Children's Problem Solving Books help children resolve social conflicts.

Research shows that the more alternatives a child can think of the more likely he or she is to display socially acceptable behavior. Elizabeth Crary's books help increase children's awareness of alternatives and possible outcomes of those behaviors.

How to use Children's Problem Solving Books —

These books are different. Each book can be read traditionally (straight through) or as a "choice" book. As a choice book, it invites listener participation. When the story come to a decision the child can decide what the character will do. The reader then turns to the appropriate page and continues with the story. The text includes questions that encourage children to consider the feelings of others.

Each book focuses on a different issue, offers several alternatives and illustrates possible consequences of those choices. Each book is $4.95.

I Want It: What can Amy do when Megan has the truck she wants? *Paper 9602862-2-5*

I Can't Wait: How can Luke get a turn on the trampoline? *Paper 9602862-3-3*

I Want to Play: How can Danny find someone to play with? *Paper 9602862-4-1*

My Name is Not Dummy: How can Jenny get Eduardo to stop calling her a dummy? *Paper 9602862-8-4,*

I'm Lost: What can Amy do to find her dad? *Paper 943990-09-2*

Mommy, Don't Go: What can Matt do when he doesn't want his mother to leave? *Paper 943990-26-2*

Written by Elizabeth Crary
Ms. Crary is the author of over ten books, among them the best-selling *Without Spanking or Spoiling: A Practical approach to Toddler and Preschool Guidance,* and *Kids Can Cooperate.* She is a parent education instructor at North Seattle Community College, and a frequently requested speaker for workshops and conferences across the United States and Canada.

Illustrated by Marina Megale
Within the simplicity of her illustrations, Marina Megale captures the depth and variety of childhood emotions. She has pictured children with both the joy and frustration involved in social situations. Ms. Megale works as a free-lance artist in Seattle.

Call Today
1-800-992-6657

See Your Bookseller
Or Write Parenting Press, Inc.

Parenting Press Inc., ■ Dept. 400, P.O. Box 15163, ■ Seattle WA 98115